HIDDEN
HISTORY
of
DAYTON
OHIO

HIDDEN
HISTORY
of
DAYTON
OHIO

Tony Kroeger

THE
History
PRESS

Published by The History Press
Charleston, SC
www.historypress.com

Back cover: Elephants bathing in the canal during a street carnival in 1899, photo by William Lutzenberger. *Courtesy of Dayton Metro Library*.

First published 2021

Manufactured in the United States

ISBN 9781467142502

Library of Congress Control Number: 2020945740

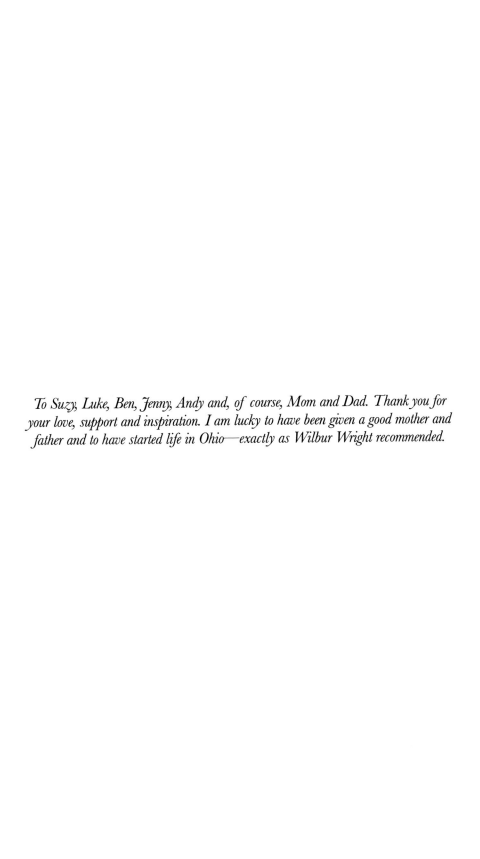

To Suzy, Luke, Ben, Jenny, Andy and, of course, Mom and Dad. Thank you for your love, support and inspiration. I am lucky to have been given a good mother and father and to have started life in Ohio—exactly as Wilbur Wright recommended.

CONTENTS

ACKNOWLEDGEMENTS

When I moved to Dayton in 2006, it was for the most practical of reasons: to work in a real city and to be closer to my family in Cincinnati. Little did I know that I would meet two of the most passionate people about their city—city planners John Gower and Brian Inderrieden. That passion extended far beyond the obvious Dayton history (although we all love that too). These were people who seemed to know it all, especially the intricacies of which I was most interested—the overlooked, the dark and the misunderstood. They selflessly took me on tours of the city and provided a sense of wonder, fascination and intrigue—the vast appreciation for the hidden history. What was just a job for me quickly became a lifetime of exploration—an endless series of mysteries to explore. To Brian and John, I am forever grateful.

I also want to thank John Rodrigue of The History Press for first reaching out about this project and for providing guidance and expertise along the way.

A tremendous source of information for this project was Samiran Chanchani of HistoryWorks, LLC. Samiran is brilliant, trustworthy and a pleasure to know—not a combination that is easy to find.

My sister, Jenny Kroeger, gave countless hours reviewing the narrative, and to her I am most grateful.

I also want to thank the Dayton Metro Library and Dayton History for being essential image sources. There is a strong sense of collaboration in Dayton.

INTRODUCTION

They put us on lists of dying cities. They took pictures of our vacant buildings for entertainment. The last Fortune 500 company departed the area, and other large companies left downtown for the newest interchange. Then the great recession hit. They wrote our obituary.

As these things happened in the first few years after I moved to Dayton in 2006, I, like many, wondered about the future of Dayton, if there was one at all.

Of course, we know that places like Dayton do not just wither away. There is too much attachment and too much to lose—inertia, if nothing else. Even in the most challenging of times, it is a wonder to look back at those events and think about where we are heading. Arelis R. Hernández of the *Washington Post* wrote on August 10, 2019, "If Dayton's heritage is ingenuity—from the Wright brothers' flying machine to metal cube trays and pull-tops of pop cans—its present is resilience." This is accurate, and the resiliency traces back further than the most recent challenges. The City of Dayton's population peaked (so far) in 1960 at 262,000. Today it stands at about 140,000. Massive suburban migration, industrial decline and globalization, redlining and racism have all brought tremendous challenges.

In 1967, Dayton architect Paul Deneau observed, "Dayton, while possibly still a little behind, is, more so than ever, a city of opportunity." I believe this is still true today, despite all Dayton has been through. One could argue that the challenges contribute to today's opportunity—this city and all its history here to be discovered. As Orville Wright said, "Isn't it astonishing that all these secrets have been preserved for so many years just so we could discover them!"

Dayton is resilient. To be sure, every city has an inherent degree of resiliency. But Dayton is particularly resilient. I think it is because of the innovation and history—both of the very prominent kind and the hidden. History is character. History is placemaking. These are the things that make a person love a city. And, as we have seen—through our recent troubles especially—Dayton is loved. A city is not just a dot on a map, it isn't just statistics or data or a ranking on some top (or bottom) ten list. It is a collection of shared knowledge and experience, the composite of events big and small.

We know that vegetation with deep roots is especially able to survive the most difficult of circumstances, like severe drought and wind. History is the deep roots of a city. And just as the plant roots are nearly totally out of sight, so is much of the history—the hidden history.

And the challenges—as tough as they can be—add to character as well. It is part of our DNA, resiliency encoded into the city. The challenges are part of this place.

In 1910, Wilbur Wright said, "If I were giving a young man advice as to how he might succeed in life, I would say to him, pick out a good father and mother, and begin life in Ohio." Why wouldn't you want to be born in a place that is resilient, strong and lovable?

The most commonly known history frames our identity. The hidden history is the connective tissue, the fabric that brings it all together. History is not just a survey of interesting things that once happened. Layered and complicated, it is composed of small things that in aggregate make a big difference. It is, of course, natural anywhere, regardless of history, for people to be connected to their home, their neighborhood and their place. Dayton is special because of this especially strong connective tissue, the deep roots that keep us in place through the worst times and in the best of times remind us of what led us here. When you experience a city—get out, walk around—really, that's how you get to know hidden history. As Toni Morrison said, "When they fall in love with a city it is for forever and it is like forever. As though there never was a time when they didn't love it."

Hidden history is the implicit character. Sometimes, it is literally hidden from sight (such as chapter 1, "Formed by the Sea, Shaped by Ice," or chapter 8, "Subterranean Dayton") or very hard to notice. Sometimes it is in the everyday environment but holds deep meaning (such as chapter 6, "Hidden Recent Past: The Midcentury"). In fact, one might not even know it is history (such as the sites of chapter 5, "The Dayton Project").

This book explores the themes and topics that one does not readily encounter, especially as time has obscured but not removed the fundamental building blocks of the city (such as chapter 3, "The Persistent Impact of the Canal," and chapter 4, "At a Crossroads"). In the same way that we should all revere the Wright brothers and Paul Laurence Dunbar, we should also be aware of the many things that in aggregate provide character, give us deep roots (such as chapter 7, "Relics of the Past," and chapter 2, "Traitors and Heroes"). Dayton did not become known for its resilience by chance. The resilience results from the stories and events that unfolded over our remarkable history—and as such, a history that contributes to the deep roots of this place.

Hidden history is found everywhere, from the oldest downtown buildings, to the urban renewal towers, to the suburban streets. I hope that this book will help develop your understanding of our shared roots and encourage future exploration.

Chapter i

Formed by the Sea, Shaped by Ice

The most hidden of Dayton historical events are those that occurred long before its founding settlers arrived. Or, in some cases, before any human activity whatsoever.

In a built-up urban environment like that in which Dayton exists, one might overlook how natural geologic events have shaped the development of the city. However, these events have determined why the city exists and persists, why it was so efficient in its development and how it will be sustained in the future. With advantageous natural waterways, an underground geologic and hydraulic bounty and scenic vantage points, the first settlers found a location with tremendous natural advantages, albeit mostly unknown to them.

The Dayton landscape we know today was born of ice—glaciers thousands of feet in height, along with the geologic material they carried and the subsequent outwash that flowed as the glaciers melted. At numerous stages within the last 1.6 million years, Ohio has been covered by this glacial activity. During the Pleistocene Epoch, glaciers that covered the Dayton area formed in central Canada. The thickness of these ice sheets caused them to flow under their weight, slowly making their way south through Ohio. The last glacier in Ohio was the Wisconsin Glacier, which reached the state about 40,000 years ago. It ultimately retreated around 10,000 years ago, but only after it contributed substantial resources.

Dayton is built over a thick deposit of outwash, particularly sand and gravel, as a result of glacial melting. After the ice fronts retreated, the outwash filled previously formed valleys with these materials. The outwash deposits in the Dayton area can exceed 250 feet in depth.

In the Dayton area, much of the topographic variation is the result of moraines from the Wisconsin Glacier, as well as kames and eskers left behind upon the subsequent melting thereof. The south part of the city of Dayton and into the south suburbs prominently features this kind of moraine landscape. For example, the elevated area containing Calvary Cemetery and the bluffs south of Carillon Park are often cited as resulting from being a glacial endpoint. While the Wisconsin Glacier reached as far south as the Cincinnati area in one advancement, the Wisconsin ice re-advanced southward in the Dayton area during its final northward retreat and in many areas deposited till on top of previously laid down sand and gravel.

A kame is a hill of sand and gravel that was deposited at the edge of a glacier or in depressions on the ice's surface. As the ice melted, the materials were lowered onto the landscape. Streams flowed along channels beneath the ice and at areas around and immediately in front of the ice sheet. In front, where slowing water spread over flat land, thick deposits of gravel and sand formed. The irregular accumulation of these materials, accompanied by the periodic advance and recession of the ice front, produced a topographically varied land surface. The first authoritative source on the geology of the Dayton area was August Foerste (1862–1936), who provided the following description of the "kame territory" of the Dayton area:

> *North of the O'Neil road* [now Dorothy Lane], *the kame territory extends at different points from more than half a mile to nearly a mile west from the Cincinnati pike* [now South Dixie Drive]. *In the Hills and Dales area it includes all of the country east of the Wayne's Pass road, as far south as the Locust farm, and the Stroop road. South of Delco Dell and the Grand View farm, the kame area extends as far as Hole's creek.*

Also due to glacial retreat, large ridges of sand and gravel, called "eskers," were formed by meltwater depositing sediment in cave systems below the ice. They represent narrow stream deposits originally supported laterally by walls of ice. When the ice melted, the linear deposits were left behind, marking the courses of the former channels or tunnels. These landforms are prevalent in the area farther south of Carillon Park. Foerste describes the following as esker territory: "The long narrow gravel ridges south of Dayton extending from Calvary Cemetery and Carmonte southward to Morane farm and Delco Dell are eskers."

The clay, sand, gravel and boulders carried by the ice contribute to the geologic wealth of the Dayton area. While kames and eskers are the result

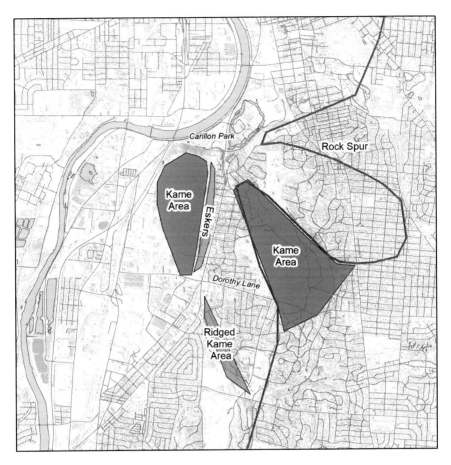

The glacial areas described by August Foerste—the kame and esker territories. *Map by author.*

of deposition in place, some of the smaller sediment particles were carried away by meltwater to form outwash deposits. Glacial outwash deposits are a major source of sand and gravel, which has become one of Ohio's most important nonenergy mineral resources. There are, in fact, still major aggregate quarries in the Dayton area, particularly north of Dayton near Interstate 70 and to the east, in Greene County.

Today's Dayton landscape has been greatly impacted by an ancient river system, the Teays, and its subsequent blockage by glaciers. The Teays River was the principal pre-glacial waterway in the region. It flowed from the Piedmont Plateau of Virginia and the Carolinas across West Virginia, Ohio, Indiana and Illinois to the Mississippi system. It entered Ohio near

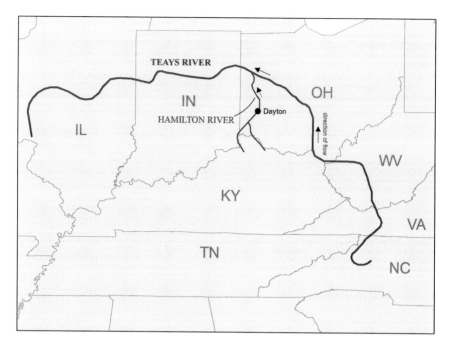

The mysterious Teays River had a major impact on the Dayton region. *Map by author.*

Portsmouth and flowed north through the vicinity of Chillicothe and then northwest past Springfield and Sidney to Indiana. The course of the Teays River ran about thirty miles northeast of Dayton. Before glaciation, the western and southern portions of Ohio were drained by this river system.

At various points along its course in Ohio, the Teays River was joined by major tributaries that, like the Teays River, carved broad deep valleys. The major valleys in the Dayton area were established, at least in part, by Teays River tributaries. One of these tributaries, the Hamilton River, flowed through a valley that would later host the Great Miami River. That is generally accepted, but this Teays River tributary leads to one of the greatest questions of the natural history of the Dayton region—specifically, in which direction did it flow?

Some geologists believe that the Dayton area was a headwaters area in the Teays time and was drained by a south-flowing Hamilton River, like today's Great Miami River. The Hamilton River, according to these geologists, joined with other tributaries that turned westward near Cincinnati and met the Teays River in Indiana. Others believe that before the formation of the Ohio River, the Kentucky River flowed northeastward through "the old Miami Valley" to a junction with the Teays River in northwestern Ohio. There is still uncertainty today about which is true. In any case, the modern Great Miami River was formed as a result of complex drainage changes of this time. In southern Ohio, the Teays River Valley ceased to be a major drainage way about 2.5 million years ago. Where this occurred, the younger streams commonly cut below the levels established in the Teays time, leaving remnants as terraces along the valley walls and, of course, deep valleys cut into the bedrock. These valleys now are filled with glacial sediment—yielding systems such as that of the Great Miami Buried Valley Aquifer.

The Great Miami Buried Valley Aquifer System stores 1.5 trillion gallons of fresh water. Its presence is the result of the glacial outwash that flowed after glacial melting, leaving behind layers of soil, sand and gravel, through which the underground water flows. Capable of providing nearly 3,000 gallons per minute to wells, the aquifer was essential in supporting the industrial development of Dayton (and sustaining industry today), leaving a legacy of industrial buildings prime for reuse.

Long before the area was covered by ice sheets, however, stones and minerals formed as a result of this area being covered by a large body of water. Approximately 430 million years ago, during the Silurian Age, the area was covered by a relatively shallow sea, encompassing the area today represented by Ohio and adjacent states. Around that time, the Ohio area was a tropical environment located about twenty degrees south of the equator. Sediment accumulated at the sea floor and became compacted into consolidated rocks. The stone that would become a key building material for Dayton was once essentially mud brought to this shallow sea by Silurian rivers. And so, the Dayton built environment, including many of its most historic structures still standing today, was formed of calcareous remains of sea organisms.

Thus, this progression of natural events led to Dayton being underlain with what would become known as Dayton Formation. The Dayton Formation is composed of dolomite and shale horizons and ranges between four and five feet thick. The Dayton Formation, also referred to as Dayton stone, Dayton marble and Dayton limestone, was quarried extensively for building stone in the Dayton area, especially during the nineteenth century. Some early researchers used the term "Dayton Formation" for the name of this stone (as opposed to, say, Dayton limestone) because the unit is not just pure limestone—the often heavy presence of the mineral dolomite, rather than calcite, precludes the formation from technically being called limestone.

The earliest settlers, and Native Americans before them, took advantage of the area's stone. Early settlers built their cabins outs of logs but used locally gathered rocks for chimneys and hearths. As communities grew, so did the use of stone, particularly for use as building foundations. The tendency of limestones and dolomites to split into layers made them suitable for the walls of public buildings like schools, churches and courthouses. The quarrying of these ancient limestones and dolomites has always been one of Ohio's top mineral industries. While in early settlement periods, people used limestones and dolomites as building stone, by the mid-1900s, people mainly used them to produce crushed stone. Many quarries are still in operation today, mostly to extract limestone aggregate. Throughout the entire time, however, lime production from limestone has been an important product as well.

Lime is made by burning limestone and using the resulting calcium oxide in mortar, plaster and whitewash. It is an important component of the chemical, farm and glass industries. In 1799, lime was made for the first time in Dayton, from stones gathered from a riverbed source and piled on a log fire, which acted as the kiln. Newcom's Tavern was the first house plastered with lime mortar instead of clay.

The underground presence of the Dayton Formation was a bounty during some of Dayton's most productive boom times. Evidence of the use of this building material is prevalent in the Dayton area in some of the most historic structures. Nearly all of the rock for some of the most historic structures came from the Dayton Formation, most intensively in the Dayton, Beavertown, Brookville and Centerville areas during the nineteenth century and early twentieth century. Some prominent examples are at Woodland Cemetery. The Woodland Cemetery office and chapel were both constructed in 1887. The main gate, office and chapel are constructed of sedimentary rocks—including the white limestone of the Dayton Formation. The Dayton Formation is laid parallel to its original layering or bedding in the wall by the main entrance to the cemetery. In some private mausoleums, large bedding-plane slabs are mounted vertically or inclined and are used for walls.

The most prominent building featuring the Dayton Formation is the Old Courthouse at Third and Main. It is regarded as one of the best surviving examples of a Greek Revival courthouse in America. The design was inspired by the Temple of Theseus. Howard Daniels, an architect and landscape gardener noted for his classic cemeteries in Ohio and New York, was recruited to replicate the design for the building—and it was then crafted from locally quarried limestone in 1850. Canal locks in the area, including the Miami and Erie Canal Lock at Carillon Park, are also made from this rock.

The chapel at Woodland Cemetery is an example of a building that features locally quarried Dayton limestone. *Author photo.*

Today's landscape reveals the former quarry locations from where this stone was extracted. One of the easiest early quarries to discern is the lake near the Lakewoods Tower at 980 Wilmington Avenue. This lake is in the place of a quarry that existed in what was then Van Buren Township (now part of Dayton). Reliable information about old quarries is remarkably difficult to find, although this quarry can be seen on the 1907 USGS Topographic Map. It has been said that from this quarry came the stones for the second Montgomery Courthouse (which was demolished in the 1970s).

Another location where a quarry existed is in Kettering, just south of Dorothy Lane along Rushland Drive. There is no surface water at this location, but an obvious depression in the landscape marks where the location from where the material for many prominent Dayton buildings was extracted. The depression is approximately two and a half acres in size. Other sites where quarries are said to have existed are at today's Cleveland Park and Belmont Park in Dayton and various sites in the Beavertown area of Kettering. In the Centerville area, quarry locations include the site of current-day Benham's Grove at 166 Main Street and the water body that serves today's Rod and Reel Club at 2190 Lake Glen Court.

This site, at 980 Wilmington Avenue, was once a quarry site for Dayton limestone. This part of Montgomery County was particularly dense in limestone quarries. *Author photo.*

This site on Rushland Drive features a clear depression in the landscape where quarry activity occurred. *Author photo.*

Oakes Quarry Park in Fairborn provides an excellent opportunity to see the area's limestone resources, which were quarried here starting in 1929. *Author photo.*

Certainly, one noteworthy use of Dayton limestone was the stone extracted from the McDonald Stone Quarry on the McDonald Farm in Greene County. It was from this location, in 1850, that the state stone—each state was asked to provide a native stone—was extracted for the construction of the Washington Monument. The stone, measuring six feet by three feet, nine inches, is located in the stairway on the interior of the monument.

Perhaps the best site to see the impact of natural events is at Oakes Quarry Park in Fairborn. The park contains a fossilized coral reef from the Silurian Period, due to the presence of the shallow sea of the time.

From an ancient sea to the Teays River and subsequent glaciers, natural events have shaped the history and the very existence of the Dayton region. It is easy to overlook the impact of these events, but now, in some cases hundreds of millions of years later, they affect daily life throughout the region. You just cannot find anything more hidden than this: ancient, unseen, but tremendously important.

CHAPTER 2

TRAITORS AND HEROES

John Cleves Symmes, a land speculator from New Jersey, initiated much of southwestern Ohio's settlement. In 1795, he sold the land containing today's Dayton to a notorious and infamous group composed of General Arthur St. Clair, the first governor of the Northwest Territory and general of the Continental army; General James Wilkinson, Revolutionary War leader and, later, "artist in treason"; Israel Ludlow, prolific land surveyor; and Jonathan Dayton, the youngest person to sign the U.S. Constitution and friend of Aaron Burr and occasional nemesis of Wilkinson.

The land became known as the "Dayton Purchase." Israel Ludlow, despite being the only one of the original landowners to come to the site and being the one who originally surveyed and laid out the streets, named the village after his friend Jonathan Dayton. The town of Dayton was initially platted on November 4, 1795. Ludlow would be the one who laid out Dayton's notoriously wide streets, which at four poles (sixty-six feet) were wide enough to "turn a coach of four." Besides Main Street, he named three of the original streets after St. Clair, Wilkinson and himself and a fourth street for Thomas Jefferson.

While a common bond—the development of the town—united this group, they experienced very divergent paths. Ludlow, among many talents, was a competent and prolific town planner. Dayton, Wilkinson and St. Clair have a different kind of legacy.

General Arthur St. Clair has a complex history—while he enjoyed his share of success, his greatest defeat is more than a footnote. He led U.S.

Army forces, in 1791, to its worst defeat ever to American Indians—it would become known as "St. Clair's defeat," alternatively the "Columbia Massacre" or the "Battle of a Thousand Slain." The defeat was to a tribal confederation led by Miami chief Little Turtle and Shawnee chief Blue Jacket, with aid coming from British collaborators. Over six hundred American soldiers died in "St. Clair's defeat." As author Carol Cartaino describes it:

> *Of Gen. Arthur St. Clair's original army of three thousand men, only forty-eight survived—a casualty rate of greater than 97 percent. Fully one-quarter of the entire U.S. Army was destroyed in a single battle—the best of the veterans of the American Revolution annihilated by warriors with antiquated weapons. This devastating loss came to be called St. Clair's Shame.*

And yet, his legacy is better than some of Dayton's other founders.

Jonathan Dayton is known historically for a variety of reasons, but for the sake of the new settlement, probably most important is that he had exceptionally capable friends in Ludlow and Daniel C. Cooper. Previously educated as a surveyor, Cooper was about twenty years old when he first went west to Fort Washington, near Cincinnati, to look after the land interests of Jonathan Dayton, including the Dayton Purchase.

While Cooper and Ludlow were initiating the development of the new settlement, Wilkinson was engaging in nationally treasonous activities. Writing in a secretive code, Wilkinson made a career of selling secrets to Spain in the wake of the Louisiana Purchase. He also secretly notified Spain of the Lewis and Clark expedition, suggesting they send armed patrols to stop them. Furtunately, they did not find the explorers.

In 1784, after the Revolutionary War, Wilkinson settled in Kentucky and became a land speculator, although he stayed busy in political activity. Seeing the strategic advantage of the Mississippi River and access to New Orleans, he engaged in an attempt to secede the western part of Kentucky from the United States and received compensation from Spain in the process. Wilkinson became aligned with Spain in 1787 and would come to be known by Spanish leaders as Agent 13. He received a pension from Spain for many years.

After prompting suspicions of treason from American leaders of the time, he curiously chose to align himself with Aaron Burr, who was already under suspicion for similar charges and also wanted for murder in New York and New Jersey as a result of his duel with Alexander Hamilton.

But even Burr underestimated the duplicitous nature of James Wilkinson, who got word to Thomas Jefferson of Burr's attempt to cleave parts of the

From the "Cyclopedia of American Biography."
Copyright, 1889, by D. Appleton & Co.

James Wilkinson, one of the primary founders of Dayton, is also known as one of the great traitors in U.S. history. *Courtesy of the Dayton Metro Library*.

Southwest away from the United States, which would become known as the Burr Conspiracy. Impressively, James Wilkinson managed to one-up a man who had a conspiracy named after him. With a history like this, it is not a wonder why Frederick Jackson Turner would call Wilkinson "the most consummate artist in treason the nation has ever possessed." Today, his namesake street in Dayton is a primary north–south arterial, two blocks from Main Street.

Jefferson's namesake street is three blocks west of Wilkinson's. Of the relationship between Wilkinson and Jefferson, author Andro Linklater says:

> *Thus the paradox running through James Wilkinson's career is the service he performed for the United States while he was unmistakably betraying it. That tortured relationship reached its peak with Thomas Jefferson, who not only confirmed Wilkinson as commander of the U.S. Army, but appointed him to the posts of governor of Louisiana Territory and commissioner of Indian affairs. No president trusted Wilkinson more, or asked so much in return, or, at the apogee of Aaron Burr's conspiracy, came closer to a catastrophic misjudgment of Wilkinson's uncertain loyalties.*

James Wilkinson wasn't the only investor in the settlement to be aligned with Burr. The man from which the city drew its name, Jonathan Dayton, was one of Burr's closest associates and worked with him in nefarious efforts. Dayton was arrested in 1807 for treason, as a result of his connection with Burr's conspiracy to overtake the Northwest Territory. While he was exonerated, Dayton's reputation never recovered.

The tumultuous relationship between Dayton and Wilkinson peaked in 1806, when Dayton created a newspaper called *The Western World* that existed to discredit Wilkinson.

The four men—Wilkinson, Dayton, Ludlow and St. Clair—had paid eighty-three cents per acre for the sixty thousand acres at the confluence of the Great Miami and Mad Rivers from Symmes. Symmes had originally agreed to pay Congress sixty-eight cents per acre, but Congress, blaming a miscommunication between buyer and seller, chose not to honor the Symmes agreement and on March 3, 1799, passed a law giving any persons who had a contract with Symmes dated before April 1, 1797, the opportunity of purchasing the land for two dollars per acre. When Symmes would not pay the higher rate, the four original proprietors also chose to waive their right to purchase the property from the government. Residents simply left instead of paying the high cost, and by 1802, only five families remained in the Dayton settlement. Dayton was doomed, and the group of men from whom it was born was of no significant help.

Daniel Cooper saved the town. After a discussion with the federal government, in 1801 he was appointed proprietor. Cooper bought three thousand acres from the federal government at the two-dollars-per-acre price. He re-platted the town using the original survey, with minor alterations. Clear titles were passed to the original settlers who were once again given an "inlot'" within the city and an "outlot." When original owners left the property, new settlers were required to pay two dollars an acre for their "outlots" and one dollar for the city lot.

Most of the early settlers of Dayton had arrived from Cincinnati. In March 1796, three parties left Cincinnati bound for the new settlement. One group, led by Samuel Thompson, selected to travel down the Ohio River, to northbound on the Miami and finally to the mouth of the Mad River at the Dayton site. The other groups, whose leaders were William Hamer and George Newcom, chose a land route. The water route proved to be the better choice, as it proved to be far more efficient.

Thompson's group arrived at the Dayton site first, specifically at the end of St. Clair Street, today part of RiverScape MetroPark. Catherine

DANIEL C. COOPER
CRAYON by HUGO FROEHLICH
FROM the PAINTING THROUGH THE
COURTESY OF ROBERT W. STEELE.

Daniel Cooper, perhaps the most important figure in the settlement of Dayton. *Courtesy of the Dayton Metro Library.*

Thompson is thought to be the first of these individuals to set foot ashore. Hamer's less fortunate party, the first to start, came in a two-horse wagon over the uncompleted Mad River Road, still being cut by Daniel Cooper.

Thompson's boat crew left Cincinnati on March 21, 1796, and arrived at the Dayton site on April 1, 1796. The land-bound travelers arrived two days later, cold and uncomfortable.

One particular family, the Van Cleve family, is especially noteworthy in the development of Dayton, playing a fundamental role in its growth. Benjamin Van Cleve was born in New Jersey in 1773 and was a young man when his father, John Van Cleve, brought the family west to Cincinnati. Benjamin was present when Ludlow surveyed Dayton in 1796 and served as the village's first postmaster, librarian and schoolteacher. The Van Cleve home was a block from the Great Miami River at Jefferson and First Streets. He taught school at Newcom Tavern, a log structure that stood at Main and Monument Streets and was moved here as a history museum until 1964, when it was moved to Carillon Park. Benjamin's son John served as mayor and led efforts to beautify the town.

John W. Van Cleve, born on June 7, 1801, is said to be the first male child born in Dayton. He became known for his literary, scientific and artistic skill and dedicated voluntary work for the improvement of the town. Says author Robert Wilbur Steele of John W. Van Cleve, "He was remarkable for both versatility and thoroughness, and might have been described in the broadest sense as an all-around man, but for a slight lack of development of the imaginative and emotional side of his nature."

Benjamin Van Cleve. *Courtesy of the Dayton Metro Library.*

The above description seems overly critical of a person who translated fairy tales from other languages and created volumes of watercolor paintings of wildflowers. Van Cleve seemed to always stand out in a crowd, and not just because he weighed over three hundred pounds. He was an accomplished musician, painter, engraver, civil engineer, botanist and geologist. Several sheets of fossils found in the Dayton Formation engraved by him are preserved at the Dayton Public Library. He established Woodland Cemetery, the third of the distinctive "rural cemeteries" opened in the United States. Named for John Van Cleve, Van Cleve Park was completed in 1892 with manicured walking paths and landscaped gardens. Dayton was in full Van Cleve reverence at the time—Orville and Wilbur Wright, who were descended through Benjamin Van Cleve's mother, named one of their bicycles the "Van Cleve." Van Cleve Park was later reshaped, enhanced and renamed Riverscape MetroPark.

While extremely important, even the Van Cleve legacy cannot live up to that of Daniel Cooper. Cooper would ultimately complete the road from Fort Hamilton to the mouth of the Mad River. Considered to be the first overland route between Cincinnati and Dayton, it opened the area for development. Cooper was very generous to the Dayton settlement. He gave either land, money or both for churches, schools, a cemetery and a park and persuaded new settlers to come to Dayton. Cooper Park is the location today of the downtown Dayton library and its adjacent green space. In the 1896 book *Early Dayton*, authors Robert W. Steele and Mary Davies Steele wrote, "It is eminently proper that the square in which the library building stands should be called Cooper Park, for the generous, public-spirited man who gave it and other valuable lots to the town." He donated the land at Third and Main for the county courthouse to be built. He operated a general store and, when troops were stationed in Dayton during the War of 1812, organized soldiers

Cooper Park and the first library at the site. *Courtesy of the Dayton Metro Library.*

to build a levee along the Great Miami River. He contributed immensely to the industrial development of Dayton, operating several mills and donating the land for the Dayton Hydraulic, which became the water power source for early manufacturing in the town.

Dayton's earliest lots are situated just south of the Great Miami River. After first being platted by Ludlow in 1795, the town plan was revised and added to several times later by Cooper. The centrally located Main Street formed the spine of this settlement. The earliest lots now form the heart of downtown Dayton. The grid of streets that Cooper mapped retain their layout, accommodating the historic transformations, with the construction and removal of buildings in the lots that compose downtown. Cooper laid out the lots to the east of Dayton in May 1815, including today's Oregon District.

Cooper also was key in development south of town, where he also purchased one thousand acres in 1798. The land contained a spring, later called the Rubicon, on which he built a gristmill and a sawmill. Cooper lived at this site until 1803, when he sold his farm to Colonel Robert Patterson, a Revolutionary War veteran and future grandfather of John Henry Patterson,

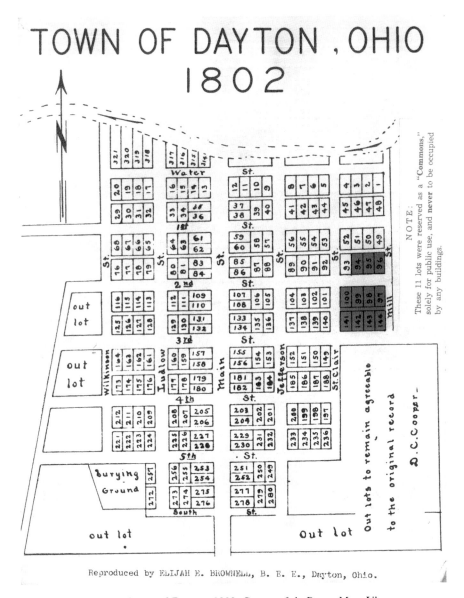

Daniel Cooper's revised map of Dayton, 1809. *Courtesy of the Dayton Metro Library.*

founder of the National Cash Register Company. The land was incorporated into Patterson's Rubicon Farm. When Cooper sold his land to Patterson, he built his stately home at the southwest corner of Ludlow and First Streets.

Cooper lived at First and Ludlow until his death on July 13, 1818. He died delivering a church bell for the First Presbyterian Church (later to become Westminster Presbyterian). When the bell for the church arrived at his store, at the southeast corner of Main and First Streets, he placed it on a wheelbarrow himself and began to take it over to the church. In retrospect, this turned out to be an uncharacteristic miscalculation, as he over-exerted himself and ruptured a blood vessel, which caused his death. His grave site is located at Woodland Cemetery.

This early period in the history of Dayton and its downtown is important in several ways. Streets and lots laid out during this period provided a foundation for future growth and development of its downtown. The commercial district was bounded by transportation routes and waterways: the river to the north and west, the railroad to the south and the canal/Patterson Boulevard to the east. Main and East Third Streets became the focus of commercial and civic activity during this period and would remain so until the post–World War II period, when the downtown underwent a significant expansion to the west. Industrial growth, commerce, retail activity and the establishment of urban institutions such as courts, schools, opera, churches, newspapers and a public library all exemplify the city's development.

CHAPTER 3

THE PERSISTENT IMPACT
OF THE CANAL

From the time the canal was first considered to its waning days before being replaced by Patterson Boulevard, Dayton grew from a quietly steady outpost north of Cincinnati to an industrial powerhouse. Because of the canal, Dayton became an essential port city, providing access for towns north of Dayton to the Cincinnati market. And yet, its time as a major form of transportation was remarkably short. The Miami and Erie Canal was not fully completed until 1845, preceding the arrival of the railroad to Dayton by only six years.

Thomas Jefferson advanced a vision for a system of waterways through the Ohio territory that would connect it to the Atlantic Ocean. Ohio governor Ethan Allen Brown established a Canal Commission in 1820, which led to the Canal Act of 1825.

The State of Ohio authorized the construction of a canal between Cincinnati and the Mad River at or near Dayton, naming it the Miami Canal. On July 21, 1825, ground was broken south of Middletown, on the Daniel Doty Farm, for the Miami Canal. Months later, one thousand laborers were hard at work on the canal, destined to reach Cincinnati and Dayton. Wages for common laborers began at five dollars per month plus board, including a daily ration of whiskey.

In 1829, the Miami Canal fully opened in between Dayton and Cincinnati. The completed Miami Canal, fed by dams and feeders from the Mad and Miami Rivers, ran for 66 miles, with twenty-four locks and ten aqueducts. Construction continued northward through the 1830s until finally the newly

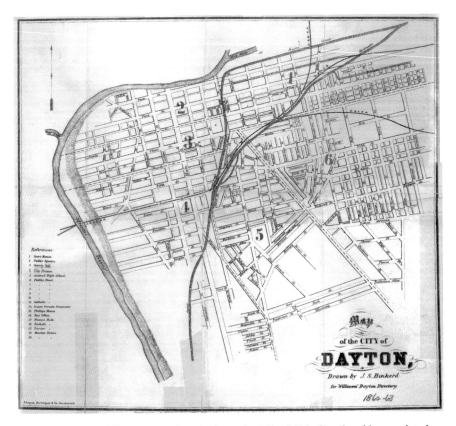

This historic map of Dayton prominently shows the Miami-Erie Canal and its associated feeders and races. *Courtesy of the Dayton Metro Library.*

named Miami and Erie Canal was completed in 1845. At 248 miles long, the canal went gradually uphill to the summit at Fort Loramie, Ohio, and then downhill to Lake Erie. In Dayton, the canal was constructed along the east boundary of Daniel Cooper's plat, with its basin on Mill Street. The location was practical because a nearby millrace built earlier by Cooper could be used as a feeder to provide water for the canal. From the basin, the canal headed south to Cincinnati, serving over sixty mills along the way.

The time between the completion of the Miami Canal in 1828 and the completion of the Miami and Erie Canal in 1845 is very important to the Dayton story. The history is well documented, but what is lesser known is the impact that it has on the built environment today. During this time, Dayton essentially became a port city. The preceding Miami Canal—the stretch from Dayton to the Ohio River—made its impact far before the canal from Lake Erie to the Ohio River was complete. Many towns to the north of Dayton found themselves in an important position in relation to the port. The cities of Troy, Tipp City and Piqua, and the farmers of that area, suddenly had access to the rest of the country. Although whiskey, flour and pork were popular shipping items, wheat and corn were also staples of the shipping industry to Cincinnati. Additionally, the residents of the interior could finally receive finished goods from Cincinnati that had not previously been available locally.

The utility of the canal led to tremendous investment. Businesses that could take advantage of this transportation achievement had a reason to locate in Dayton—and they arrived to a degree that would transform the region. Over seven thousand passengers arrived in Dayton from Cincinnati in 1831. Towns that were located along the canal saw tremendous benefit from their sudden good fortune. Dayton's population increased from about three thousand at that time to about twenty-five thousand by 1857. The Dayton port activity was bustling—also in 1831, Dayton shipped 59,550 barrels of flour, 5,602 barrels of whiskey, 563,000 pounds of bacon and pork and 334 barrels of linseed oil. In one year in the late 1870s, over 33 million pounds of ice cleared the port of Dayton.

Access to the rivers helped trade and the construction of mills in the years following its settlement in 1796. Roadways and transportation routes in Ohio were rudimentary during the early nineteenth century. The canal not only provided a vital trade route for Dayton to export and import agricultural and other products; along with its branches, the canal was also a source of hydraulic power that fostered the growth of mills and early industry in Dayton. Commerce, before the arrival of the canal, was centered on Main Street and Third Street, which was an early turnpike linking the city to nearby communities. The canal was a boon for the development of Dayton, with hotels, saloons and retail emerging near the basin, which formed a boundary between the commercial district to its west and the industrial district, later known as Webster Station, to its east. This bustling activity created great change in Dayton's urban environment. For one, it caused a shifting of the most active area from the Main Street corridor eastward to the canal basin.

With the establishment of Cooper Hydraulics in 1838 near Fifth and Wyandot Streets, the canal became a resource for commercial hydraulic power. In addition to existing mills near the rivers, new mills and factories opened farther south between Third and Sixth Streets. These establishments included the Osceola and Oregon Mills, the Cooper Cotton Factory and the Sachs-Prudens Brewing Company. By the late nineteenth century, the

Items located along the canal ready for shipment. *Courtesy of the Dayton Metro Library.*

banks of the canal were lined with industrial plants. Among the industries in Dayton that relied on hydraulic power was the large Barney and Smith Car Works, located northeast of the basin. Barney and Smith was second only to Chicago's Pullman Company in manufacturing railroad cars. Ironically, the company used the power harnessed from the canal to help propagate the railroad, which contributed to the demise of the waterway itself.

From the mid-nineteenth to the early twentieth century, Dayton's industrial district thrived along the Miami Erie Canal between First and Sixth Streets, which included early buildings such as mills and warehouses along the canal. The industrial district continued to prosper through the mid-twentieth century, with companies such as the Dayton Engineering Laboratories Company (Delco) making important contributions to the development of the automobile.

Even after the railroad replaced the canal as the main mode of long-distance transport, the canal and the hydraulics provided power to the many flourishing mills and industries in Dayton. Canal Street was lined with warehouses, small factories and shops, as illustrated by the 1887 Sanborn Fire Insurance Map.

Not only did the main artery of the canal shape Dayton as we know it today, but the canal feeders and races did as well. A fitting analogy situates the canal as the interstate highway, with various on/off ramps coming off it.

Locks were used to raise and lower boats from one elevation of land to another. Three large feeder lakes provided a fresh supply of water to the canal: Grand Lake St. Marys, Lake Loramie and Indian Lake.

By 1875, however, the railroad had replaced the canal, putting it on a rapid path to obsolescence. The Miami Erie Canal was significant in promoting trade and commerce for Dayton by providing an effective way to ship goods. Yet by the time it was completed in 1845, it was already facing competition from a faster and more efficient means of transportation—the railroad. The first railroad track to be laid in Ohio was between Toledo and Adrian, Michigan, in 1836, nine years before the canal reached Lake Erie at Toledo. The first railroad in Dayton, connecting it to Springfield, opened in 1851. Cincinnati, Hamilton and Dayton Line was the second railroad to be operational that year, with other railroad companies rapidly laying their tracks in Dayton in the coming years.

Even as the canal lost its dominance for trade and transportation after the arrival of the railroad, it remained a catalyst for the city's industrial growth through much of the nineteenth century, with mills and manufactories operating on hydraulic power along its banks.

Tolls collected from boats on the Miami Erie Canal declined steadily after the construction of the railroad. By the 1870s, the Dayton-Cincinnati segment of the Miami Erie Canal was the only section that remained profitable. The profits came from the mills and factories using the canal for power. Most of the earlier mills have been replaced by later development; however, remaining buildings such as the Sachs-Prudens Brewing Company at 120 South Patterson Boulevard and the warehouse buildings at Patterson Boulevard and First Street continue to provide testimony to mid-nineteenth-century Dayton.

The Miami Erie Canal fell into disrepair during the late nineteenth century. Discussions of its abandonment proliferated during the early 1900s, with John Patterson, founder of the National Cash Register Company and former canal toll collector, lending his voice to that cause. After much debate, the State of Ohio began to repair and rebuild large sections of the canal, replacing basic infrastructure such as locks and aqueducts. Replacement of the disused Miami River Aqueduct began in 1906 but was abandoned in 1912 due to a lack of funds. The canal era came to a sudden end with the destruction caused by the flood of 1913.

By the time of this image in 1912, the abandonment of the canal was a foregone conclusion; the flood of 1913 made it certain. *Courtesy of the Dayton Metro Library.*

It was an unceremonious ending for the canal, losing usefulness due to the rise of the railroad and then left as a blighted open sewer before being removed. In 1925, the Miami Erie Canal was officially abandoned for transportation purposes, although portions remained in use until 1940 for hydraulic power generation. Plans to fill much of the canal to make way for the Miami Canal Parkway came soon after the canal was abandoned. By 1927, the State of Ohio had passed legislation authorizing the purchase of all properties required for the construction of the road. The filling of the canal began in 1928. Existing, unfilled segments of the canal had taken on the appearance of open sewers as they waited to be built on. The parkway, which was eventually named Patterson Boulevard for National Cash Register founder John Patterson, opened in 1938.

The impact of the canal is visible today and, in some ways, growing. What is now known as Webster Station was the industrial powerhouse of the region, and it took on a built form that can still be witnessed today. Many of the industrial buildings are still on the landscape and are being converted to new uses, especially as new housing developments.

Buildings directly related to the canal (today, Patterson Boulevard), just south of East First Street. *Courtesy of the Dayton Metro Library.*

These buildings on Patterson Boulevard just south of East First Street are the most intact examples remaining of canal buildings. The canal-era usage was primarily warehousing. *Author photo.*

Four buildings directly associated with the Miami Erie Canal Basin in the Cooper Park area remain standing in the present day, located between East First and East Second Streets. In 1887, the buildings housed the A.W. Nixon Tobacco Warehouse, the Miller Brothers Cigar Factory and a grain warehouse. Located farther south on the block, the fourth remaining structure was, in 1887, a lumber and produce storage facility. The Dayton Engineering Laboratories Company (Delco) was founded in 1909 by Charles Kettering and Edward Deeds and is best known for pioneering automobile innovations, such as the anti-knock fuel additive and the electric ignition self-starter switch. In 1915, Delco built a large research, production and office building at 335 East First Street. Delco also used older buildings in the vicinity as research and office facilities. Research for the fuel additive occurred at the A.W. Nixon Tobacco Warehouse at 144 Canal Street. The success of Delco brought other businesses, including the General Motors Frigidaire plant, to the district.

The path of the canal can be observed in the scale of the streets that were built along its route. The following roadways took the place of the canal or canal feeders: Burns Avenue, Patterson Boulevard and Rita Street, for example. These are particularly wide roadways, some with a boulevard

Roadways like Rita Street that replaced the canal are easy to spot due to their oversized width. *Author photo.*

The remains of the aqueduct that carried the Miami Erie Canal over the Mad River. *Author photo.*

Aqueduct carrying the Miami Erie Canal over the Mad River. *Courtesy of the Dayton Metro Library.*

median. Additionally, all of these rights-of-way contain large storm sewer infrastructure beneath them, as contemporary infrastructure was installed in the drainage system that the canal came to represent.

Buried into the flood levee on the south side of the Mad River is a former aqueduct abutment. Curiously out of place on the otherwise natural mound of the levee, the limestone abutment is an interesting remnant of this transformative transportation project. Aqueducts, constructed of masonry and wood, were built to carry the Miami Erie Canal over rivers and streams along its path. They typically comprised a water channel to carry the canal boats and an adjoining path for mules to tow the boat. Nineteen aqueducts were constructed in the complete Miami Erie Canal. One of these aqueducts carried the canal over the Mad River in Dayton and was located to the northeast of Patterson Boulevard, between Keowee and Findlay Streets. The aqueduct was built in 1833, during the first phase of the extension of the Miami Canal northward to Lake Erie. It was destroyed by the Great Flood of 1913 in Dayton, together with much of the remaining infrastructure of the canal in the city.

CHAPTER 4

AT A CROSSROADS

The impact of being located on early paths, roads and turnpikes is an overlooked component of Dayton history—mostly because these roads retain only hints of their pre-interstate-era roots. Today, their presence has been obscured, but signs of them remain for those who look closely.

Two of the most important pre-interstate roads in the country passed through Dayton, and in neither case was Dayton's inclusion originally part of the plan. Significant lobbying and shrewd strategy were necessary to put Dayton on these major routes. The Dixie Highway and National Road put Dayton on the map of the most important roads of the time. However, they were preceded by earlier routes that helped shape the city.

THE EARLY ROADS

Most of the early roads in the area connected Dayton to points south. The first of these connected Hamilton to Dayton. The "Hamilton Road" followed the Great Miami River around Franklin and past Miamisburg. Then the road proceeded northeast, to the site of today's Dayton Mall and then north to where South Dixie Drive and West Schantz intersect. The road turned northeast through the land that became Oakwood, along the future West Schantz Avenue. It then proceeded north on a road that is

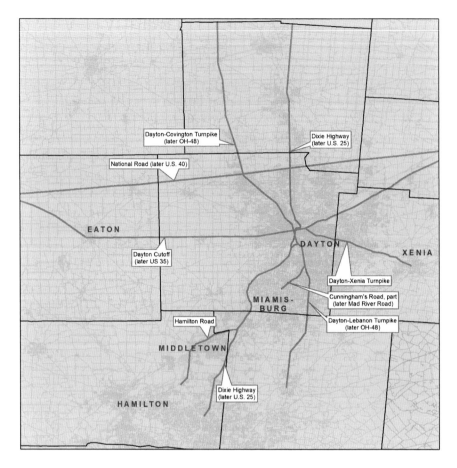

This map shows the development of early roads to and through the Dayton area. Dayton's development was facilitated by its inclusion on such roads. *Author photo.*

now Brown Street to Dayton. The same path was eventually followed by a later road, the Cincinnati Pike, which extended the reach of the Hamilton Road to Cincinnati.

According to the Ohio Historical Marker near the subject road, the first overland route connecting Dayton to Cincinnati was described as the "Road from Cunningham's to the Mad River." (Later, it was more commonly known as Mad River Road.) It was surveyed and established in the late 1790s by Daniel Cooper, Daniel Griffing and John Hole. "Cunningham's" was an early settlement to the north of Cincinnati—it was an extension of Harmer's Trace north from near Cunningham's Station in the Mill Creek area to the mouth of the Mad River in the Dayton area. This was the route that Dayton's earliest settlers used. The segment between David Road and State Route 725 is the last remaining traceable portion retaining this name. Then the road ran northbound for another 3.5 miles. This northern segment was a forerunner to the Lebanon Turnpike and later Far Hills Avenue, but the original survey was to the west of the current roadway on a line that would have entered Oakwood about two blocks west of its current location, finally joining Far Hills Avenue at approximately where Oakwood High School stands. It would then follow the course of the present road to join the Hamilton Road on the way to Dayton.

Several turnpike companies were chartered to build macadamized (compacted broken stone) roads connecting Cincinnati to Dayton. One of the resulting roads was the Great Miami Turnpike, constructed in 1840, which would later be parts of Cincinnati-Dayton Pike, Dixie Highway, U.S. Route 25 and South Dixie Drive.

THE DIXIE HIGHWAY

Dayton's prominence was facilitated by being on the Dixie Highway, but it took quite a bit of lobbying to be included on the route. Carl Fisher was the person who established the Indianapolis Speedway and formed the Lincoln Highway Commission, which built the first drivable highway across the United States. He is also credited as being the figure behind the establishment of Miami Beach, Florida, and the Dixie Highway.

The "Dixie Highway" name became official on April 3, 1915, when the Dixie Highway Association was formed in Chattanooga, Tennessee. Naturally, Illinois, Indiana, Kentucky, Tennessee, Georgia and Florida were represented at that meeting, as those states would have to be crossed on a course from Chicago to Miami. But Ohio representatives were present as well, on behalf of the effort to include the state on the route. Ultimately, Ohio was successful. The highway would split at Indianapolis, with one branch heading south through Louisville, while the other followed the National Old Trails Road east to Dayton before turning south through Cincinnati and Lexington. Upon that split and several additions thereafter, the Dixie Highway evolved into a network rather than a singular route. Downtown Dayton became the junction point of a Dixie Highway connector road. The Dixie Highway system would go on to include several connector roads between the north–south branches of the highway.

Kodachrome by C. H. Ruth

U. S. 25, on site of Old Canal, Dayton, Ohio—84-D-37

Patterson Boulevard/U.S. 25. *Courtesy of the Dayton Metro Library.*

After Patterson Boulevard replaced the Miami Erie Canal in Dayton, U.S. 25 was relocated to Patterson Boulevard around 1940, meeting the original Dixie Highway at the Schantz Avenue intersection in Oakwood.

South of Dayton, the Dixie Highway alignment passes through cities including Moraine, Kettering, West Carrolton and Miamisburg. In some locations, it takes on alternate names, such as Kettering Boulevard and Central Avenue, and also in segments it becomes a one-way couplet where the directions of traffic are significantly separated. Through all of these stretches, the route claims dense commercial activity, no doubt facilitated by its roots as the primary means of north–south traffic through the area.

During World War II, when Frigidaire switched from producing refrigerators and began wartime production of airplane parts, bullets and machine guns, Dixie Highway in Moraine received additional lanes and an extension due to the heavy volume of truck traffic shipping war supplies.

The Dixie Highway, later incorporated into U.S. 25, remained the primary long-distance north–south route through the area until it was replaced by Interstate 75.

THE NATIONAL ROAD

In 1802, the federal government promised to provide Ohioans with a road that connected the soon-to-be state with points east of the Appalachian Mountains. The National Road was one of the first paved (compacted gravel) roads to cross the Appalachian Mountains. The United States Congress authorized the construction of the National Road in 1806. In 1811, Congress awarded contracts to private builders to construct the road. The War of 1812 prevented work from beginning until 1815. Construction began in Cumberland, Maryland, and the contractors completed the road to Wheeling, Virginia (modern-day West Virginia), in 1817. From 1825 to 1838, the National Road was extended across Ohio.

As the road was brought westward, the mandate was to build a road directly from one state capitol to the next. In doing so, many existing communities found themselves off the path of the National Road—including Dayton, which would be located about ten miles south of the straight-line path. East of Columbus the city of Newark had been missed and Dayton was determined to avoid that fate. By the time the National Road reached central Ohio, it was clear that it carried a major advantage in providing a direct link to eastern markets, especially since the new canals across the state ran north and south. As surveying for the road neared, Dayton officials proposed a diversion through the city, via a slight southward bend. This alternative route, they argued, would intersect the new Mad River and Erie Railroad line, and would provide access to industry. A route directly west from Springfield, on the other hand, would primarily traverse open farmland.

However, all of their efforts were nullified when President Andrew Jackson overruled the recommendations of the Ohio legislature and ordered that the road be built straight and without detour through Dayton. When state legislators presented their appeal for a diversion to Washington, President Andrew Jackson decided, on legal grounds, that the road would follow the prescribed Springfield to Richmond route. The result was that like Newark, Dayton was bypassed by about ten miles. Dayton leaders had another idea.

The city quickly built their road from Springfield to Dayton, then west to Eaton and then northwest to Richmond, Indiana, where it rejoined the official National Road. The "Dayton Cutoff" connected Springfield, Dayton, Eaton, and Richmond. When the National Old Trails Road Association chose its path across the country, it went the path of the where the better-quality roads existed, and that was through Dayton, about ten miles south of Vandalia and the National Road.

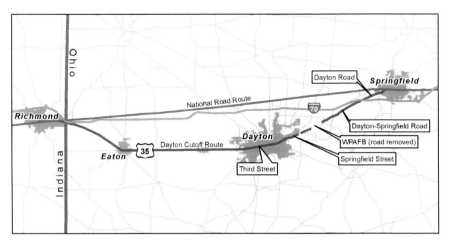

Map showing the route of the Dayton Cutoff in context with the National Road and current Interstate 70. The Dayton Cutoff route was five miles longer but was popular due to the better road conditions. *Author-created map.*

Dayton erected milestones along its alternative road that were nearly exact copies of the milestones found along the National Road. At the fork in the road, the cutoff's proponents had a sign erected telling travelers that the fork to the *left* was the National Road, when in fact it wasn't. Most importantly, the Dayton Cutoff enjoyed great success because it has a better road surface. It also passed through two larger communities (Dayton and Eaton; the northern option only had tiny villages) and merchants with whom travelers could conduct business. These advantages were able to make up for the Dayton Cutoff being five miles longer—the Dayton route is fifty-eight miles between Springfield and Richmond, while the intended National Road route is fifty-three miles between the two cities.

Because of these efforts, the Dayton Cutoff claimed substantial traffic from the National Road for the next eight decades. Just west of downtown Springfield, the Dayton-Springfield Road intersects U.S. 40. This was one of several roads—Ohio 4, Lower Valley Pike, New Carlisle Pike and Brandt Pike were others—that would link the official National Road to Dayton. Perhaps most notable is a road that still maintains the given title—National Road in Beavercreek, between Kaufman Road and Colonel Glenn Highway, which is most certainly not part of the official National Road. An Ohio transportation survey reported that the official National Road from Brandt to the Indiana border remained "unimproved" gravel, stone or cinder-covered road and that most through traffic still detoured through Dayton and Eaton. Travel guides took travelers along the Dayton Cutoff rather than the official

U.S. 35 west of Dayton, the extension of Third Street, was also the route of the earlier Dayton Connector. Being located on a major east–west route gave rise to businesses oriented to travelers. *Author photo.*

The Capri Motel was built along the Dixie Highway. It was designed by Dayton architect Paul Deneau. *Courtesy of Cardboard America.*

National Road. Only 240 vehicles used that section of the road each day in 1925, compared to 3,400 on the section from Brandt to Springfield.

The National Road did improve transportation and communication between the frontier and the East Coast, which increased Ohio's population. Most Ohioans, however, continued to rely on the Ohio River and Lake Erie to send their goods to the major markets of the eastern United States. The National Road's importance declined with the advent of canals in the 1820s and 1830s and with railroads in the 1840s and 1850s. Modern-day U.S. Route 40 follows the National Road's original route.

The Cincinnati, Hamilton and Dayton Railroad was the first to reach Dayton in 1851. Other railroad companies, including the Dayton and Xenia Railroad and the Dayton and Michigan Railroad, soon began operating from Dayton. The passenger station was located near Sixth and Jefferson Streets; the railroad lines running in the east–west direction shaped the southern boundary of downtown, just as the Miami Erie Canal and its basin had set its east boundary.

Dayton managed to position itself as a primary juncture point on very important networks, including the National Road and the Dixie Highway. The impact of these turnpikes persists beyond their impact in the development of the region. Persisting land uses are very much a part of this hidden history. Midcentury hotels, built before the interstate system, still dot the landscape. These are, in fact, the most persistent and in some ways the primary means to recognize the importance of the transportation giants of their time.

Great examples include the former Capri Hotel on Dixie Drive (now Budget Inn), the Red Horse Inn on Dixie Drive and two budget hotels on Dixie Drive in Dayton, near Harrison Township. Former and current auto fueling and service stations persist, as does the architecture typical of that time.

OTHER CONNECTING ROADS

Linden Avenue in Dayton became the starting point for the Dayton and Xenia Turnpike, which connected to two towns before the construction of U.S. 35. The other end of the former turnpike is Dayton Street in Xenia. Between the two, it retains the appropriate name of Dayton-Xenia Road. The first segment of the Dayton and Xenia Turnpike was completed in 1858.

The Dayton and Covington Turnpike would, in Dayton, become North Main Street, known as OH 48 since 1921. This was a toll road, with construction beginning in 1839, following the route of the Stillwater Road and the earlier Native American Stillwater Trail. The Dayton and Covington Turnpike was completed in 1841. Some sources say that a building at 120 North Main Street in Englewood was a tollhouse associated with the turnpike.

CHAPTER 5

THE DAYTON PROJECT

C ontained within the atomic bombs dropped on Hiroshima and Nagasaki was a triggering mechanism that initiated a series of reactions that would change human history forever. The triggering mechanism used radioactive polonium and was developed at secret sites in Dayton, Ohio.

This crucial component of the nuclear bomb development program known as the Manhattan Project was the Dayton Project. The event that brought this project to Dayton was when Charles Allen Thomas and Carroll Hochwalt formed Thomas and Hochwalt Laboratories in Dayton in 1926. Their first office was located at 127 North Ludlow Street. The duo created a series of successful products, which prompted the Monsanto Chemical Company to buy the Dayton company. It would become the company's Central Research Department, with Thomas as director.

In 1942, the U.S. Army Corps of Engineers assigned the Monsanto Chemical Company with the responsibility for the development of radioactive polonium-210, which would become an essential component of the atomic bomb. The Dayton Project began in 1943 when Monsanto's Thomas was recruited by Manhattan Project leaders to coordinate the plutonium purification and production work. Scientists at the Los Alamos Laboratory calculated that a plutonium bomb would require a neutron initiator. To this end, Monsanto's subsequent research, development and production activities would occur intensively at several Dayton sites.

The best-known neutron sources used radioactive polonium and beryllium. The radioactive isotope polonium-210 (Po-210) is one of twenty-five known radioactive isotopes of polonium, and it specifically would become the focus of the Dayton work. Po-210 is, by mass, one of the deadliest toxins—about 250 times more deadly than hydrogen cyanide. Thomas sought to produce polonium at Monsanto's laboratories in Dayton. While most Manhattan Project activity took place at remote locations, the Dayton Project sites were uniquely situated in a densely populated urban area.

In 1943, Monsanto used its Central Research facilities at 1515 Nicholas Road in Dayton to organize the polonium project and recruit scientific personnel for the program. The facility was subsequently designated as Dayton Unit I. Though Po-210 was never produced or refined at that particular facility, scientists did perform spectrographic and X-ray work on polonium and developed the refinement process that would be used later, at Unit III, according to *Polonium in the Playhouse* author Linda Carrick.

Unit II was the Monsanto Rocket Propellant works off Betty Lane near Ohio State Route 741 in Miami Township. While it was administered by Monsanto, it would not end up being actively used by the Dayton Project. The site handled explosives, including ammonium nitrate and ammonium picrate, but no radioactive materials were handled there. Work at Unit II ceased in the fall of 1945. Its not being used for the Manhattan Project was reconsidered in December 1946, but this proposal was rejected in favor of constructing an addition at Unit III. Today the site is a suburban residential subdivision. An estimated twenty-seven thousand vehicles drive by the site daily, with the occupants unaware of what nearly occurred there.

In 1943, Monsanto leased a three-and-one-half-story building at 1601 West First Street from the Dayton Board of Education. This site would become Unit III of the Dayton Project, known as the seminary site. The building was constructed in 1879 by the Church of the United Brethren as a home for seminarians attending Union Biblical Seminary (now the United Theological Seminary), which had been established under the vision of Bishop Milton Wright, the father of Orville and Wilbur Wright. The building was sold to the Dayton Board of Education in the 1920s and served as the Grace A. Greene Normal School. When the Dayton Project took over, the space had last been used as a book warehouse and was in bad shape; the windows were broken, and the staircase between the second and third floors was missing.

The building had to be extensively renovated to accommodate the project's chemistry, physics and electronics laboratories. New heating and lighting

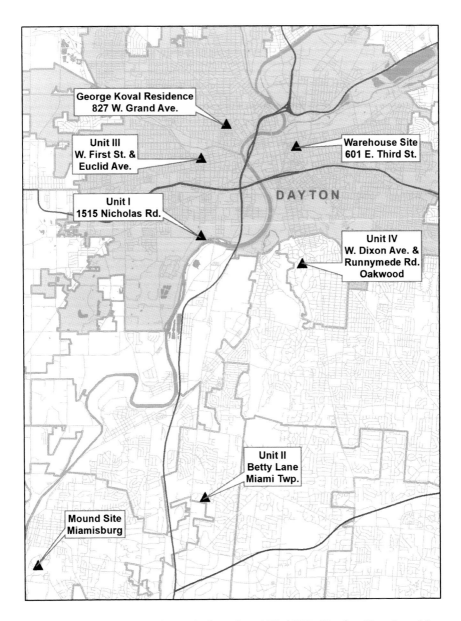

Map showing Dayton Project sites and other selected World War II–related locations. *Map by author.*

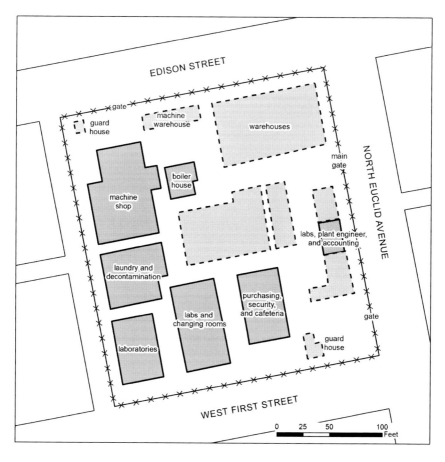

This map shows the locations of buildings during the polonium development effort. Many of the buildings are still standing today in Dayton's Wolf Creek neighborhood. *Map by author.*

A 1947 image of Unit III of the Dayton Project at Edison and Euclid Streets. *U.S. Army photo.*

The remaining buildings from the top-secret site in Dayton's Wolf Creek neighborhood where polonium was developed for use in the U.S. nuclear program. *Author photo.*

were installed, windows were replaced, new flooring was installed and rooms were re-plastered. This main building provided six thousand square feet of laboratory space on two floors, with an additional three thousand square feet available on the third floor.

Over time, many ancillary buildings were added to the site outside of the main building, including a chemical storage shed, a clinical laboratory, two guardhouses and a security fence, a counting room for measuring radioactivity, glassblowing and machine shops, offices, a cafeteria, locker rooms, a physics laboratory and a laundry facility.

The site was near downtown Dayton, in the middle of a working-class neighborhood, today called the Wolf Creek neighborhood. It eventually grew to encompass twenty buildings covering approximately two acres. Writing for the *Dayton Daily News* in 2016, Timothy R. Gaffney put it in perspective: "It just so happened that Unit III's research work, so crucial to making an atomic bomb, took place just half a mile from where the Wright brothers had invented the means to deliver it."

The Dayton Unit III site was used for the research, development, processing and production of polonium and the storage of processing residues. Two processes were used to obtain polonium-210. The first process involved the extraction of Po-210 from lead dioxide wastes generated by the Port Hope radium refinery in Ontario, Canada. A total of 73,774 pounds of lead dioxide wastes were received and processed by the Dayton Project, with the first shipment arriving in November 1943. The second process, found to be superior to the lead dioxide process, involved the chemical separation of Po-210 from bricks and slugs containing bismuth-209. Once the methods for irradiating bismuth and separating polonium from the irradiated bismuth had been developed, virtually all polonium purified at the Dayton Project was prepared by this method.

Almost weekly, a large truck carrying hundreds of bismuth slugs would arrive in Dayton from Oak Ridge, Tennessee, where the slugs had already been irradiated via neutron bombardment. Workers at Unit III were tasked with separating the polonium using acid extraction methods and assembling the triggers for the atomic bomb.

In 1948, this project component was moved to Mound Laboratories in Miamisburg, Ohio, and all operations at Dayton Unit III ceased in 1949. Discontinuing activities at Unit III would lead to the designation of Unit IV, the Playhouse location, at Runnymede Road and Dixon Avenue in Oakwood. In 1950, the Unit III site was returned to the Dayton Board of Education. At the time of its return to the board, several buildings were left at the seminary site, including the original, renovated seminary building, which was later demolished by the board of education. Also, after the transfer, an additional building (Building 7) was constructed on a portion of the concrete pad that formerly supported a laboratory building referred to by Monsanto as the Quonset hut.

The Dayton Project also included the "Warehouse" site, which was located at 601 East Third Street. In May 1945, Monsanto rented three floors of the building here from General Electric. Between 1946 and 1949, the Department of Energy (DOE) used a portion of the Dayton Warehouse for Manhattan Project activities. Initially, it was used to receive and store equipment used by the project. Ultimately, three floors of the building were used for storage, the fourth floor served as office space and the fifth floor was used as a health physics laboratory, where bioassay, biomonitoring samples and polonium's effects on laboratory animals could be studied and tested away from contamination from other polonium sources. Today, the site, located in the rapidly redeveloping area of Webster Station, is a target for redevelopment.

The polonium-based neutron initiators were used in both the gun-type Little Boy and the implosion-type Fat Man used in the atomic bombings

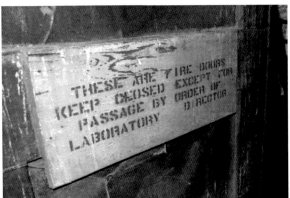

Above: The Dayton Warehouse site at 601 East Third Street (2020). *Author photo*.

Left: This sign was photographed inside the Unit III building at 601 East Third Street, noting the use of the fifth floor as a laboratory for the research of polonium. *Author photo*.

of Hiroshima and Nagasaki, respectively. The fact that polonium was used as an initiator was classified until the 1960s—but far earlier, George Koval, a technician with the Manhattan Project's Special Engineer Detachment, penetrated the Dayton Project as a spy for the Soviet Union. What nobody in the Dayton Project knew was that they had developed the polonium process not only for America's nuclear weapons program but also Russia's.

George Koval was the son of Jewish Russian immigrants who was drafted into the army, where his scientific talents led to his assignment as a health physics officer for the Manhattan Project. He worked first at the Oak Ridge site in Tennessee and later at the Dayton Project. Koval was also a Moscow-trained Soviet mole, having spent years in Russia—a part of his past he somehow managed to conceal. Koval was one of several Soviet spies who penetrated the Manhattan Project, according to news reports. But his Dayton espionage was most crucial because it yielded the technical details on how to use polonium in bombs and how to make it. The polonium secrets took years off the Soviet Union's bomb program, and its first test in 1949 shocked Western countries. Koval slipped back to Russia in 1946 and died in obscurity in 2006. His work as a spy only came to light in 2007, when Russian president Vladimir Putin awarded him the posthumous title of Hero of the Russian Federation. When working for the Dayton Project, George Koval lived at 827 West Grand Avenue, a home still standing today in the Dayton View neighborhood.

Unit I, on Nicholas Road, continued to be used by Monsanto as an administrative facility until 1988, when it was demolished. The land was sold to Quality Chemicals in 1992 and then to DuPont in 2002. Unit III, the seminary site, was decontaminated in 1950 and returned to the Dayton Board of Education. The original seminary building was subsequently demolished, but several structures remain from the Dayton Project. The site is now listed in the National Register of Historic Places. The seminary site is surrounded by a chain-link fence with barbed wire. The three existing gates are at the same locations as the three gates used by Monsanto for access to the property during the Dayton Project.

Although the lease on Unit IV, the former Runnymede Playhouse, specified that it was to be returned, it was determined to be too contaminated. The building was demolished in February 1950. Even the cobblestones in the driveway were removed, along with several feet of of earth from under the structure. The excavation was filled in, and the site was returned to the Talbott family, who were paid $138,750 in compensation. As of 2017, all that remains of the original playhouse is a brass doorknob and part of the greenhouse roof, which are part of the collection of the Mound Science and Energy Museum. Private residences now occupy the site. The Dayton Warehouse was decontaminated in 1950 and returned to its owners. The Mound Laboratories continued to produce polonium initiators until 1969. Polonium continued to be produced there for commercial sales and use in satellites until 1972. The laboratories were decommissioned in 1993, and the area was decontaminated. It now houses the Mound Advanced Technology Center.

In 1996, the Department of Energy, which had succeeded the Atomic Energy Commission, decided that since the Dayton sites already had been decontaminated, they did not warrant inclusion in the Army Corps of Engineers' Formerly Utilized Sites Remedial Action Program (FUSRAP). However, Dayton was concerned that the cleanup did not meet modern environmental standards. Therefore, the State of Ohio asked the United States Congress to have the U.S. Army Corps of Engineers conduct a review, which was carried out in 2004 and 2005. The review concluded that no radioactive contaminants were found that would warrant inclusion in FUSRAP.

Chapter 6

HIDDEN RECENT PAST

The Midcentury

Dayton, in many ways, has a well-documented history: The Wright brothers, Charles Kettering and John H. Patterson are well known in Dayton and beyond. Similarly, Dayton has architectural gems of which the city has long been proud. But there is an emerging story that is hidden by these older, prominent topics—the more recent, but no less important, midcentury time period—the recent past that must be addressed in historical context.

Like most American cities, Dayton has many buildings constructed during the midcentury period—those built between about 1946 and the early 1970s. They are prevalent in the skyline and apparent in just about any downtown streetscape. While they may not carry all of the grandeur of eras prior, these structures, and the people who built them, are a major component of the Dayton story. It is the story of the battle for the long-term relevance of downtown Dayton, a time of fear and a time of aggressive development, struggling to secure the future of the city's core.

From a development perspective, this was a very nervous time in downtown Dayton. New malls in the suburbs were constructed, and offices began to follow. Interstate 75 was completed through Dayton in 1966, and Interstate 675 was already being planned. The wave of suburban momentum was a major cause of concern for downtown boosters.

Large redevelopment projects were seen as one way to address the problem of a threatened downtown, and a primary tool for this was urban renewal. In a series of projects designed to remove seemingly outdated buildings

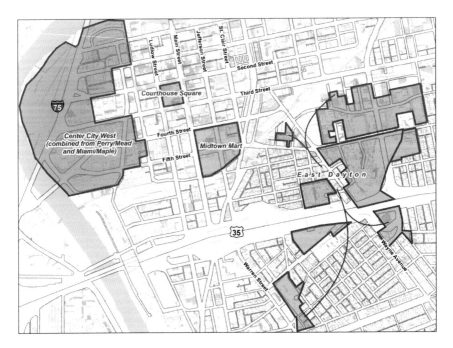

Early urban renewal areas in downtown Dayton. *Map by author.*

and construct a modern city, urban renewal transformed Dayton on a scale that no other development era can match. The projects would include the Miami-Maple and Perry-Mead Urban Renewal projects (which would be combined to form the Center City West Urban Renewal), Midtown Mart and Courthouse Square.

These projects are often criticized today for what was lost—and plenty was lost, notably densely built blocks of commercial and residential buildings. However, these actions were a product of a desire to secure the future of downtown, however imperfect the strategy. What history has been provided for this era tends to focus only on what was removed, simplistically characterizing leaders of the time as careless demolition fanatics. However, this was a time for which there was no American model for how to react to the swift expansion of suburban areas while the urban area was deteriorating.

Federal actions of the 1940s and 1950s facilitated projects of this nature. The Federal Housing Act of 1949 and the Housing Act of 1954 led to urban renewal programs in cities throughout the nation. These legislative acts provided funds for "slum clearance" associated with urban renewal projects. The Federal Highway Act of 1956, which provided federal funding for the construction of highways, gave cities incentive to complete large infrastructure projects of this kind. These acts were timely for Dayton and its trajectory. By the late 1950s, Dayton was prepared to utilize urban renewal and highway construction to address the emerging challenges of urban blight, suburban competition and dominance of the automobile. When your primary tools are urban renewal and highway development, every problem looks like an urban renewal or highway project.

In 1957, Dayton leaders embarked on a new Central Business District Study. The study showed a keen awareness of the mounting problems. In a sobering account of the situation, City Planning director Robert A. Flynn noted, "A number of problem situations are now appearing on the scene: with the river to the north, the railroad to the south and intensive industrial development to the east, opportunities for growth are limited to either vertical growth or westward growth; some deterioration is apparent in some sections; competition with suburban development; decentralization of retail activity; traffic congestion; transit routing and delays; parking—on-street and off-street; one-way streets; redevelopment." This analysis would set the tone for the efforts that would follow.

Dayton city leaders believed that the future of downtown Dayton would be secured by the removal of old buildings and the construction of high-rise structures to retain density while making room for parking and open space. This would occur while facilitating the construction of expressways in blighted areas to better connect the city to suburbs. Dayton established an Urban Renewal Department in 1957 to facilitate federal funding to acquire and clear blighted areas identified in the comprehensive plan and other studies and to redevelop them. East Dayton, a large area south of East Third Street extending to present-day U.S. 35 and east of Oregon to Keowee Street, was the first approved for urban renewal funding in 1957. This project would be followed by urban renewal projects during the 1960s and 1970s, including Center City West, Midtown Mart and Courthouse Square.

City leaders of the time noted that the western part of downtown was facing different issues from the eastern part. The eastern part, in their opinion, was more stable, and more incremental improvement was planned. However, the western part of downtown, especially to the south of Third Street, needed massive, sweeping change. The first urban renewal programs enacted in downtown Dayton targeted the geography west of Wilkinson Street. Approved in 1961, the Perry Mead urban renewal project focused on clearing and redeveloping several blocks in western downtown and expanding the central business district. The area had primarily been densely

East Dayton Urban Renewal Area: Fifth Street before demolition. *Courtesy of the City of Dayton.*

East Dayton Urban Renewal Area: Fifth Street after demolition. *Courtesy of the City of Dayton.*

The 1970s vision for the Center City West urban renewal area. *Courtesy of the City of Dayton.*

built-up single- and two-family dwellings and modest retail and business establishments. Just a year later, in 1962, the Miami Maple urban renewal project was approved by the federal government. The two adjoining project areas were eventually combined to be renamed the Center City West urban renewal project, setting downtown Dayton on a bold course in the name of modernization.

The idea of redeveloping the Center City West area was considered in the city's 1954 Comprehensive Plan, which foresaw large-scale building demolition and replacement with civic buildings and an expressway. Ultimately, an ambitious project that included not only government buildings but also high-rise apartments, a sports arena, a convention center and hotels was developed for the area during the early 1960s. The city again advanced the need for a civic center composed of government and public buildings. Complementing these civic projects were private endeavors to construct modern buildings with state-of-the-art facilities. Dayton's prominent developer Arthur Beerman, for example, constructed eight buildings in the area. However, demolition efforts proved far more efficient than building efforts. While demolition moved ahead rapidly, new construction progressed more incrementally (and at a much smaller

The Center City West vision, including a large arena. *Courtesy of the City of Dayton.*

scale), with elements of early plans only partially completed. The plans for a convention center/sports arena complex never materialized, and ultimately the locating of Sinclair Community College south of West Third Street ended the potential of the original plan—in retrospect, a rather fortunate development.

The construction of Interstate 75 and the transformation of U.S. 35 to a limited-access highway facilitated suburban competition. The concept of an expressway connecting Dayton to its north and south suburbs had been considered at least since the comprehensive plan of 1954. The "U.S. 25 Expressway," as it was then called, was to be constructed bordering the Perry Mead and Miami Maple urban renewal areas. Constructed farther west and roughly following the path of Dixie Highway, Interstate 75 bypassed the urban renewal areas. U.S. 35 followed the east–west path of the Dayton Xenia Turnpike south of the central business district. Civic leaders had believed the highways would bring distant residents to downtown. Conversely, however, the primary impact of these highways was to drive up the growth of suburban communities and to draw away retail and other functions that planners and the city's business community had expected to thrive in the business district. The concurrent development activity in downtown resulting mainly from private endeavors was already reshaping downtown in ways that would be a prelude to urban renewal. During the 1950s, Dayton's businesses and private developers led the construction of new buildings in the West First Street vicinity, west of Ludlow Street, which had previously been occupied by smaller residential dwellings.

Dayton also wanted to locate and develop a government/civic center. While plans for such a cluster of buildings were long considered and proposed at several locations, the clearance that occurred on the west part of downtown brought about new opportunities. The five-story, stone-clad Neoclassical/International-style Dayton Safety Building, which houses the city's police department, courts and the city prosecutor's office, was constructed in 1955 as the first of a planned group of civic buildings in the block. Other civic buildings followed, including the Federal Courts Building and the Montgomery County Administration Building. The Brutalist Federal Courts Building was designed by GBBN Architects and the New Formalist county building by the architectural firm of famed midcentury architect Edward Durrell Stone. Located about one block north of the Safety Building at 348 West First Street is a building that was built in 1956 to house the board of education. It was designed by Dayton's Freeman A. Pretzinger. As an October 3, 1967 *Journal News* article, "County's Building Plan Has It All," depicted, plans for a Government Plaza complex of modernist high-rise buildings in the center city area included a cluster of county and city administrative facilities, along with other office/commercial buildings. Together with the nearby city hall, courthouse, police headquarters and county jail, these buildings form a cluster of civic buildings.

There are eight existing downtown office/commercial buildings constructed during the period of 1945–59. One notable building of these is the Miller/Dayco Building at 333–49 West First Street. Considered to be a state-of-the-art modern building when it was constructed in 1957, the Miller Building was designed to have a helicopter landing pad on its terrace and underground parking for about two hundred cars. The adjacent three-story brick structure at 349 West Second Street was completed in 1960, also in the minimalist International style. Important tenants included Aetna Life Insurance, Traveler's Insurance, General Precision Equipment and North American Aviation. The Talbott Tower was a twelve-story expansion of the existing Art Moderne–style building constructed in 1937–38. These large multi-tenant buildings with modern amenities showcase the plan to better compete regionally.

Other commercial buildings constructed in the area include the three-story International-style building at 225 West First Street that was constructed as the Stratford Motel. Located at 224 North Wilkinson Street, near its intersection with Monument Avenue, is the three-story modernistic Beerman Building with a glass curtain wall extending its corner entrance bay. The building was constructed in about 1955 by developer Arthur Beerman.

BUILDINGS OF THE MIDCENTURY

Notable buildings of the midcentury time period:

Miller Building (333 West First Street)—Completed: 1957. Architect: William McCabe. Current use: redevelopment project

Talbott Tower (131 North Ludlow Street)—Original building completed in 1938; tower addition completed in 1958. Architect: Lorenz and Williams. Current use: office building, ground level retail.

Stratford Motel (225 West First Street)—Completed: 1958. Architect: Paul Deneau. Current use: office building.

Stratford Motor Hotel/Stratford House/First Place Apartments (330 West First Street)—Completed: 1962. Current use: residential apartments.

IBM Building (33 West First Street)—Completed: 1966. Architects: Shaw Metz Associates, Hugh A. Lagedrost and George E. Walter. Current use: office building.

111 Building (111 West First Street)—Completed: 1968. Architect: William Rump. Current use: office building.

Grant-Deneau Tower (40 West Fourth Street)—Completed: 1969. Architect: Paul Deneau. Current use: redevelopment project, likely mixed-use.

Winters Tower/Stratacache Tower (40 North Main Street)—Completed: 1970. Architect: Lorenz and Williams. Current use: office building.

Senior Citizens Center/Senior Resource Connection (105 South Wilkinson Street)—Completed: 1970. Architect: Richard Levin. Current use: senior center.

Transportation Center Garage/Oregon Garage—Completed: 1972. Architect: Brown and Head. Current use: parking garage.

Convention Center (22 East Fifth Street)—Completed: 1972. Architect: Deneau and Kleski (later addition by Levin Porter Associates). Current use: convention center.

120 West Second Street—Completed: 1972. Architect: Harry Weese. Current use: office building.

Montgomery County Building (451 West Third Street)—Completed: 1972. Architect: Edward Durrell Stone, with Brown and Head. Current use: county offices.

Sinclair Community College—Completed: 1972 (core campus). Architect: Edward Durrell Stone, with Yount, Sullivan and Lecklider. Current use: community college.

Mead Tower/KeyBank Tower (10 West Second Street)—Completed: 1975. Architect: Lorenz and Williams. Current use: office building.

Homestead Savings and Loan (33 East Second Street)—Completed: 1975. Architect: Levin Porter Associates. Current use: office building.

Federal Courts Building (200 West Second Street)—Completed: 1975. Architect: GBBN. Current use: federal courts.

Courthouse Plaza Southwest (10 North Ludlow Street)—Completed: 1976. Architect: Lorenz and Williams. Current use: office building.

Gem City Savings Building (6–8 North Main Street)—Completed: 1980. Architect: I.M. Pei with Lorenz and Williams. Current use: office building.

It housed offices of the Beerman companies, as well as the local offices of national corporations including Boeing.

In the 1960s, the City of Dayton found its population declining for the first time. Aging residential and commercial buildings continued to be seen as a major challenge, while the suburbs saw the construction of massive retail developments and nearby office parks. This suburban migration was leaving behind a built environment that seemed old, antiquated—built for a previous time. A 1964 redevelopment study led by the Dayton City Plan Board noted, "The loss of economic vitality in the mid-50s has brought physical obsolescence and decay in the mid-60s. The empty storerooms, the gradual deterioration of structural conditions, lack of maintenance and economic obsolescence of buildings has been apparent and is becoming more evident each year." Of particular concern was the area south of Third Street, which, according to the study, "has experienced Dayton's most serious problems of decentralization. This area historically has been the concentration of small retail merchants and thus the development of the automobile-oriented suburban shopping center has had its most serious effect on this portion of downtown."

Dayton's leaders had established a preliminary long-term plan for Dayton's central business district. The study identified that the core of the business district, which stretched along Main and Jefferson Streets earlier in the twentieth century, had expanded west to cover Ludlow Street and begun to grow farther west along West First Street with the construction of office buildings during the 1950s. City planners believed that the business core could encompass the entire downtown area over the coming decades even as it faced competition from suburbs. Setting the tone for the preliminary plan, the City Plan Board asserted, "Dayton's Central Business District (CBD) must…have a positive, conscious plan for redevelopment. Lack of such a plan can only mean ineffectual, desultory stabs at the CBD's great amorphous enemy, the outlying shopping center," according to Peterson's *Graphic Presentations of Dayton's CBD*.

During the early 1960s, planners focused on retaining the older, high-value blocks of downtown while expanding the boundaries of the district via urban renewal to add commercial and civic facilities. As the decade progressed, Dayton leaders saw that they were fighting a losing battle against suburban growth, which had benefited further from highway development. By the late 1960s, Dayton's economic struggles were visible in downtown as businesses and industries that were once cornerstones of the city relocated to suburbs and other cities. A bolder approach, with large-scale renewal and urban development projects planned for the very heart of downtown, took hold; to retain economic vitality, it was thought that even the prime areas of downtown would need to be modernized.

This was the essence of an urban development pivot point in 1968. The notion of an economically sustainable downtown evolved from interstate-oriented development to a Main Street focus. This was promoted in part by the vity bringing in national planning consultants RTKL from Baltimore. The belief emerged that without a strong Main Street corridor, downtown Dayton is a lost cause. From this vision arose a series of projects that would impact the city's central spine from the 1960s through the present day. From this vision arose some of the most ambitious redevelopment projects in Dayton's history. The consultants determined that downtown needed bold action. One particular section by RTKL's economist profoundly asks, "Will Downtown Move (or Has It?)." The report states:

Already South Dayton Mall (SDM) is anticipated to overshadow the present CBD retailing function. SDM will have 2.2 million sq. ft. of retail space consisting of 106 stores. Downtown Dayton presently comprises approximately 2 million sq. ft. with Rike's Department Store accounting for 600,000. Adjacent to the SDM are an additional 168 acres already zoned for commercial use. Some of Dayton's existing merchants are estimating that 40% of their total sales will be generated at SDM. This may, in fact, be a conservative estimate.

The SDM is expected to obtain many of the dollars now going to Tri-county and downtown Cincinnati. In addition, the SDM location is one that is central to the high income residents of the region and is perceived as a safe retailing environment by its prospective customers. Thus, it appears that with the completion of SDM, an important component of the retailing function has already moved south.

Office buildings are already locating in nearby areas adjacent to the mall. A million-dollar building is programmed to be built southwest of the Highway 41 and 725 intersection. The $8 million NCR training/office complex is currently under construction. In addition, many smaller buildings such as the Shell Oil Company regional office headquarters, the three-story $1.5 million office building located near the Imperial South Motel are in varying stages of development.

The County Planning Commission has zoned 113 acres to the east of SDM for commercial use. There have been numerous requests for rezoning the areas immediately north of SDM from south 725 to Yankee Street. The *areas directly south of the SDM are either being held for speculation (an underdeveloped half-acre lot adjacent to the mall is already valued at $79,000) or are in the process of being studied for high-density commercial planned unit development. Thus, while the office space function is still most strongly associated with downtown Dayton, large office parks are bound to be built in the next five to ten year period provided that center city creates no counter trends.*

A sub-consultant for RTKL continues:

"To put this very simply, we have seen a great deal of evidence in the questionnaires that we have been sending out and the work we have done to indicate that only a few financial decision makers are actually committed to doing their expansion in the Dayton CBD. Much office expansion can take place elsewhere in the region or it can take place in the CBD. We have seen in other parts of the country a development of large regional retail centers which then induce the development of financial office space."

The RTKL plan called for the redevelopment of Dayton's downtown to be carried out in six stages, through the 1970s. The plan proposed significant new construction within the business core, starting with the redevelopment of the old courthouse block, located in the heart of the business district between Second, Third, Main and Ludlow Streets. The city obtained funding for the Courthouse Square urban renewal project in 1973. Office towers would be constructed along Second and Ludlow Streets, while the old courthouse, at the intersection of Main and Third, would be preserved. The former Elder Beerman Store at 34–40 West Second Street and the Mead Tower were constructed as part of the Courthouse Square urban renewal project. The Mead Tower is a twenty-seven-story building with elements of the Miesian style. Constructed in 1975, the building was designed by Dayton's prolific architectural firm of Lorenz and Williams. A public plaza would be constructed between the towers and the courthouse. With Courthouse Square as the core, the phased development would extend in all directions to include department stores and retail, parking lots, additional office buildings and residential buildings located to the north, near Monument Avenue. Progress at Courthouse Square Plaza would continue later, with the construction of the Dayton Power & Light Headquarters Building at 2–14 North Ludlow Street in 1976. These features were to be connected by raised pedestrian walkways, thus creating pedestrian circulation at a second level above the streets.

While much of the RTKL plan for downtown development in Dayton did not come to fruition, Courthouse Square Plaza, which was the first stage of the development, retained the basic scheme that was proposed by the firm. The efforts are described below:

> *In late 1966 a variety of important actions were underway in Dayton's Central Business District. The new freeway, I-75, had just opened in December 1966, land acquisition in the Center City West Urban Renewal Area was approximately complete; Mr. Beerman had been awarded the contract for the redevelopment of Center City West approximately 20 months previously and two small buildings were under construction; property acquisition was just getting started for the Mid-Town Mart Renewal Project; Sinclair Community College was searching for a site; and Dayton's obsolete stock of office space provided an obvious potential for several dramatic additions to Dayton's skyline....*
> *...Many people in the community recognized the potential for coordinating this development to maximize near future downtown growth and change and direct into a cohesive growth.*

Two blocks south of Courthouse Square was the Midtown Mart urban renewal project, which had obtained federal approval in 1966. Under the direction of the RTKL plan, the Midtown Mart plan brought the focus of redevelopment efforts back to the downtown core and prioritized clearance of structures south of Third Street and east of Main Street, leading to what would become, after a shopping center plan did not materialize, the Dayton Convention Center and a landscaped park called Dave Hall Plaza and, more recently, the Levitt Pavilion.

Feasibility studies for the redevelopment of the Midtown Mart area had been carried out in 1963–64 in preparation to submit the project to the federal government for urban renewal funding. This project called for clearing four blocks, containing about one hundred buildings, located between Fourth and Sixth Streets to the north and south and St. Clair and Main Streets to the east and west. The early plans did not include a convention center; instead, they had focused on the expansion of retail, commerce and housing to meet the challenges posed by suburban growth. As early as 1964, the impact of suburban development was causing serious concern. A Midtown Mart Feasibility Report noted that development was especially challenged south of Third Street, stating that the "development of the automobile-oriented suburban shopping center has had its most serious effect on this portion

The Midtown Mart area—bounded by Main, Jefferson, St. Clair and Stone Streets—before demolition. *Courtesy of the City of Dayton.*

The Midtown Mart area after demolition. *Courtesy of the City of Dayton.*

The vision set forth for the Midtown Mart urban renewal area, which then included a hotel, apartments and plenty of retail. *Courtesy of the City of Dayton.*

of our downtown." Plans for the renewal of the Midtown Mart area were based in part on the consequences of highway construction—transportation improvements made access to suburban areas convenient enough that this area faced even tougher competition.

The City of Dayton, in the meantime, hired the architectural firm of Deneau, Kleski and Associates to identify a site and develop plans for a new convention center. The architectural firm identified the Midtown Mart as the most favorable for the abundance of cleared land and the low cost of acquisition. It was to be constructed at the intersection of Fifth and Main Streets, occupying an entire block. Plans for a second block, to be developed with private funds, were developed concurrently with the construction of the convention center. The city picked Deneau, Kleski and Associates as architects to develop and submit architectural plans for the convention center in June of that year. However, the Midtown Mart area had by then been only partially cleared, and new construction would not begin until the early 1970s. Even so, plans drawn up during the 1960s

THE WORDS OF PAUL DENEAU

Dayton architect Paul Deneau was a reporter's dream—what you see is what you get. These are some of Deneau's more noteworthy quotes:

"There's a great opportunity here for anybody who chooses to be competent in his chosen field. Because there are too many people sitting back on their fat asses."

"I don't think that I am accepted. I think I'm resented by a lot, as they would resent anyone who's doing anything. And there are some who would like me swept under the rug."

"The greatest ideas I've ever heard aren't carried out, because people don't know how or they are too lazy."

"Dayton, while possibly still a little behind is, more so than ever, a city of opportunity."

On Dayton: "I'm not ashamed to say I love this city. I dearly love it."

were instrumental for the future development of the Midtown Mart site. The plan for the Midtown Mart urban renewal area included not only the publicly funded convention center but also privately funded office towers, parking and associated facilities. As finally approved, these plans called for the construction of a transportation plaza and garage, as well as a hotel. The transportation plaza originally included bus and train stations. This would become the Transportation Center.

The modernist Convention Center opened in 1972, the same year the Transportation Center was completed. The Brutalist-style Transportation Center extends across Fifth Street and occupies almost two blocks. The building was designed by the architectural firm of Brown and Head as part of the Midtown Mart urban renewal project. The convention center underwent a façade remodel in about 2000, resulting in the removal of the original free-standing colonnade and plaza for the new metal-frame rotunda entrance. The extent of the alterations meant that the building would be considered non-contributing when much of the surrounding downtown was listed as a district in the National Register of Historic Places in 2019.

An enclosed walkway over Fifth Street was built to provide a pedestrian connection to the planned hotel. The pedestrian bridges across Fifth and Jefferson Streets that connected the Transportation Center garage to the hotel and convention center represent a partial realization of the RTKL plan, which envisioned such pedestrian bridges connecting buildings across downtown. The Transportation Center was constructed soon after. The hotel, which was constructed in 1976, occupied only a quarter of the northwest block. The remainder of the block was landscaped as Dave Hall Plaza, a public space designed by Brown and Head architects and landscape architect James Bassett of varied topography and a sunken "living room" area. A *Dayton Daily News* article from 1976 found it to be quite an achievement:

> *Contractor I.F. Weber has contoured the park's scenic ups and downs, carved its streams and pools, hauled its waterfall boulders from near Fostoria—all to Jim Bassett's picky specifications, even to the size of each rock. Siebenthaler's, award-winning landscaper of the Convention Center, is doing the planting here, too, at the site officially known as Dave Hall Plaza, Block 2.*

John Brown, of Brown and Head Architects, described the vision: "It's a downtown gateway park. Out of the bustle on Main. Short-range, we focus on the core garden and on greening the whole block. Long-range on private development at three parcels at the outer edges with landscape walkways glass enclosed as in Minneapolis and Toronto."

Outside of the urban renewal projects, modern high-rises (both as part of urban renewal projects and as stand-alone development) were constructed to replace the dilapidated and substandard commercial spaces of the past. The first of these high-rises came toward the end of the decade with the construction of the Grant-Deneau Tower.

By 1969, urban renewal efforts were well underway, and large swaths of the city had been dramatically altered, if not cleared entirely. But the Dayton skyline had not changed significantly until the construction of the Grant-Deneau Tower.

The Grant-Deneau Tower project was established in 1966 with the purchase (and subsequent demolition) of the RKO Keith Theatre. From its

Dave Hall Plaza under construction. *Courtesy of the City of Dayton.*

A fresh and new Dave Hall Plaza in the 1970s. *Courtesy of the City of Dayton.*

beginning, the building was to have a clean, modern look while exhibiting "a dash of romanticism," leading to what is now considered a Miesian/New Formalist design. The project naturally received a great deal of attention, not just because of its location, prominence and scale, but also because it was seen as downtown Dayton's counterpoint to the modern alternatives emerging in the suburbs. The Grant-Deneau Tower was the pioneering effort to revitalize downtown Dayton and compete regionally. In a 2010 study titled "Ohio Modern: Preserving Our Recent Past," consultants for the State Historic Preservation Office concluded, "The new skyscraper symbolized the conviction of Dayton's leadership that downtown was still a viable commercial center, despite relocation to the suburbs beginning in the 1960s." The development represented the belief that a strong offense of large-scale projects would make downtown competitive with the suburbs. A 1967 article in the *Dayton Daily News* states, "Above all, the construction is a statement of confidence in downtown Dayton, the region's urban core. The confidence is justified. Many have known that all along. The new project will make it apparent to all." Just one year earlier, the newspaper had noted, "The project runs counter to a trend of announcements by Dayton firms of plans for new construction away from downtown and in several cases, outside the city." The new tower was to lead Dayton into a new, modern era. The front of the sales brochure for the tower proclaimed it was "destined to be the landmark office building of the new Dayton." Years later, architect Paul Deneau would tell reporters that he believed the completion of the Grant-Deneau Tower heightened confidence in the city center and hastened the construction of the high-rises that followed. A news article from 1970 shows agreement:

> *Some, including* [Dayton Chamber of Commerce vce president Marvin] *Purk, see signs that the "new downtown" is emerging now. He pointed to new buildings such as the Grant-Deneau Tower, the Winters Bank Building, the Herman Miller Building, Rikes garage and the Holiday Inn, and commented: "We have started a trend that will accelerate."*

Upon construction, the 331-foot Grant-Deneau Tower was the tallest in Dayton. There had not been a commercial high-rise constructed since 1938 and no modernist high-rise in the city's history. The New Formalist tower dramatically changed the downtown landscape, and the city and its business leaders hoped that, along with the urban renewal projects, downtown Dayton would see new life as a result of the modern changes.

DAYTON (GRANT-DENEAU TOWER)

Completed in 1969, the Grant-Deneau Tower was the tallest in the city when it was completed. *Courtesy of the Dayton Metro Library.*

In a 1973 special section of the *Dayton Daily News* about the opening of the Dayton Convention Center, Jim Nichols reports that the convention center "joins the Sinclair Community College, the 22-story Grant-Deneau Tower, the 30-story Winters Tower, and the 22-story First National Bank building in proclaiming Dayton is alive and serving its people." On April 9, 1969, ground was broken for what was and remains the tallest building in Dayton. Designed by local architects Lorenz and Williams, the Winters Bank Building is thirty stories tall and tops out at 405 feet. It reflected state-of-the-art design. Eugene Kettering, son of Charles, believed that the building would be a driving force to entice businesses to remain and locate in downtown Dayton. Though Eugene died before construction was completed, Virginia Kettering saw the project through to the end. After Winters Bank closed, the building was renamed Kettering Tower in honor of the Kettering family. In 2019, the name would change to Stratacache Tower, reflecting new building ownership. The tower has a bronzed anodized aluminum exterior with bronzed solar glass and full-length windows.

Another major development of this period was the relocation and expansion of Sinclair Community College to the Center City West urban renewal area. The seven core buildings of Sinclair Community College were completed in 1972, although the school originated in 1887 when the Dayton YMCA offered a men's night school program. Ground was broken on August 19, 1969, for the new site. In 1967, Edward Durrell Stone was selected to design the campus, which would be located on the western edge of downtown Dayton on twenty acres in the Center City West urban renewal area. The Dayton firm of Yount, Sullivan, and Lecklider assisted Stone's firm. Stone's design for Sinclair Community College is a cohesive unit of seven buildings encircling a central plaza that attempts to create a modern equivalent of a collegiate quad to provide an oasis of calm in an industrial city. The arrangement of buildings and their almost classical simplicity show the compositional formality typical of Stone's work from this period. At the same time, the campus also displays an architectural style known as Brutalism, evident in the materiality, massing and details of the concrete buildings.

The individual campus buildings are characterized by vertically oriented end towers, with columns of recessed windows between the solid mass of the towers. The style of these buildings provided Sinclair, a new institution, with an image of permanence and strength. Although the overall campus has grown to twenty buildings, it is remarkably intact, from a historical perspective. Later buildings added to the campus are of similar design, scale and materials, especially the ones just east and west of the historic core. The original seven buildings and integrated landscaped plaza look similar to how they looked in 1972.

Dayton's architectural and planning firms—such as Deneau and Kleski Associates, Brown and Head Architects and Levin Porter Associates—

made valuable contributions in developing and realizing plans associated with urban renewal, and nationally well-known entities such as RTKL, Edward Durrell Stone and Harry Weese made their mark in the city for the first time. Even as the groundwork for the significant public and private development that would be realized later, during the 1970s, was laid, new buildings contributed a modern skyline. These buildings often replaced older buildings that had stood on the same lots. These skyscrapers were joined by other, more modest buildings, including the 111 Building, First Place Building, 369 West First Street Building, the new AT&T Building and other modernist commercial buildings elsewhere in downtown. Many of these buildings had associated parking lots created by demolishing adjacent buildings. They were like those constructed during the 1950s in that few had any retail accessible directly from the street. Two buildings stand out as different in their relationship with public spaces. The twenty-one-story 130 West Second Street Building was constructed in 1972, designed by Harry Weese Architects from Chicago. The twenty-seven-story Mead Tower and the DP&L Building in Courthouse Square, constructed in 1975 and opened in 1976, were also designed by Lorenz and Williams. The buildings have commercial storefronts accessible from the street and Courthouse Square, representing a later attempt to encourage vibrant public spaces.

Very much needed new public open spaces, including Courthouse Square, Dave Hall Plaza and those associated with the Federal Building and the Montgomery County Administration Building, were created through the efforts of this time. The period helped fulfill, although in a piecemeal fashion, the historically felt need for a "civic area" in Dayton, with the construction of the Federal Building, Montgomery County Building, courthouse and other public buildings near the existing city hall on Third Street.

First and Second Streets continued to be a focus of building activity through the 1960s. Among the buildings constructed during this time are the Ohio Bell Building, the 111 Building, the IBM Building, Price Brothers Headquarters and Stratford Motor Hotel. The Ohio Bell Building, located at 300 West First Street, was constructed in 1968. The four-story building is of reinforced concrete construction finished with brick veneer and vertical strip windows. The eleven-story 111 Building was designed by William Rump and built by the Miller family, who had earlier constructed the Miller Building and its addition at 333–49 West First Street. The IBM Building located at 33 West First Street was constructed in 1966 for the IBM Corporation. Designed by the Chicago-based architect Shaw Metz

The Stratford House is now First Place Apartments. *Courtesy of the City of Dayton.*

Associates, with Hugh A. Lagedrost and George E. Walter of Dayton, the ten-story-tall building is of concrete and steel construction with stone-faced walls. The Stratford Motor Hotel (later, Stratford House, Ramada Inn and presently First Place Apartments) was constructed at 330 West First Street and was completed in 1962 with its distinctive usable patio with kidney-shaped pool.

From 1970 to 1975, six commercial buildings were constructed on Second Street. These buildings, which signaled the significance of Courthouse Square as a focus for redevelopment, include the Elder Beerman Department Store at 34–40 West Second Street, the Mead Tower at 10 West Second Street, the Winters Tower at 40 North Main Street and the Homestead Savings and Loan Association Building at 33 East Second Street. Located only a block away from this cluster of buildings is the twenty-two-story 130 West Second Street Building. The building, designed by Harry Weese Associates of Chicago, was constructed in 1972. Completed in 1970, the thirty-story-tall Stratacache Tower is the tallest in Dayton and was designed by Lorenz and Williams. Located across the street from Kettering Tower at 33 East Second Street, the Homestead Savings and Loan Association Building is faced with a steel curtain wall. The building, which was constructed in 1974, was designed by Levin Porter Associates, its geometry and reflecting surfaces expressed in a clean, sculptural form.

Despite this intensive building activity, mid-twentieth-century city leaders had envisioned grander schemes for downtown than were realized. That these plans were only partially realized has a broader significance, in that it ensured that historic buildings from earlier eras dating back to the mid-nineteenth century remain standing side by side with the modern buildings, sometimes occupying entire blocks that remained largely unaffected by mid-twentieth-century endeavors.

The period also saw the construction of buildings with a wide range of uses, including office towers, parking facilities, a church and a medical facility. Mid-twentieth-century architectural styles—International, New Formalist, Miesian and Brutalist—are represented in buildings constructed during the period. Modest buildings constructed during the time also represent the use of modernistic elements, materials and construction techniques. The use of pre-cast concrete panels, metal, glass, curtain walls, brick and concrete trellis and decorative finishes all represent the impact of modernism on architecture from the time.

Until about 1969, most of the buildings were constructed to replace single dwellings or small retail establishments; the construction of the Grant-Deneau Tower foreshadowed the removal of larger buildings associated with commerce and social life in downtown. While significant demolition from urban renewal projects was already underway, only modest effort at new construction in cleared areas was underway at the time. During the 1970s, however, large buildings such as the Winters Tower, the new Elder Beerman Store and Mead Building on Courthouse Square, the Dayton

Convention Center and the Transportation Center replaced buildings that together occupied entire city blocks, revealing the significant impact planning initiatives and private efforts had on downtown architecture.

Evidence of this development offensive very much persists today. It exists in the buildings that were central to the development effort of the time, such as the Sinclair Community College Campus, the Grant-Deneau Tower, the Kettering Tower and the IBM Building. While at a glance these towers do not appear to express a rich heritage or architectural distinction, the truth is, they are important to the Dayton story, overlooked by many. While many of the buildings might not appear especially extravagant to the average observer, they are indeed architecturally significant. They display the common architectural themes of the time, such as Miesian modern and New Formalism. Above all, they express Dayton's story: the struggles and opportunity—and the characters behind them.

The IBM building was constructed at 33 East First Street in 1966. *Courtesy of the City of Dayton.*

Aside from the individual buildings, the urban renewal areas have the opportunity to be the strong connective tissue between the more prominent buildings of earlier eras. In fact, by their nature, urban renewal areas have a relatively high amount of open space and a relatively lower density that can be used to highlight some of the taller, more significant buildings.

Contemporary times have generally been good to the downtown urban renewal areas. Sinclair Community College is one of the largest and most-respected community colleges in the state. Dave Hall Plaza, the heart of the Midtown Mart plan, is now home to the Levitt Pavilion, featuring fifty-plus music performances from renowned musicians on a state-of-the-art stage.

And while Courthouse Square has only seen incremental improvement in recent years, it is easy to see how a fundamental redevelopment of this public space would facilitate the reaching of downtown's potential. That potential, the driving force of the massive midcentury investment, persists to this day.

Chapter 7

Relics of the Past

C lues to the past are everywhere in today's landscape. But these portals to history can be difficult to see or can exist in plain sight yet remain overlooked. Let's peel back the layers of time to see what relics of the past exist in the city today.

Potter's Field

Located beneath a thick tree canopy south of Woodland Cemetery and north of the Patterson Park ballfields on Irving Avenue is a location once designated as the final resting place for the city's destitute. It is quite difficult to find evidence that it even exists. While difficult to find, there are circular stones marking locations in the potter's field. A potter's field is the burial ground for those who were unable to afford other burial space. This is not the more well-known potter's field in Woodland Cemetery. The other—more plainly visible—ground of this kind is located just north of Stewart Street. It was the first of three potter's fields in Dayton; aside from the two in the Woodland area, the third is located on Gettysburg Avenue on the western side of the city. This one lies in a secluded wooded area between baseball diamonds.

Bridges to Yesterday

At several places in Dayton, you can find physical remnants such as vertical slabs of concrete suggesting a former crossing over a river or roadway. Locations with these features include the former railroad overpass over Patterson Boulevard (just north of Stewart Street), the remaining abutment from the canal aqueduct over the Mad River (near Dayton Children's Hospital), the former Williams Street bridge over the Wolf Creek, the former Bridge Street bridge over the Wolf Creek and a remote bridge abutment over the Stillwater River near Wegerzyn Gardens MetroPark.

Abutments are the part of the bridge that connect to the embankment and carry the weight of the deck superstructure. They sometimes remain after the removal of the bridge due to the cost to remove them and, in some cases, to maintain the stability to the ground behind them. Their presence, and the absence of their associated bridge, illustrates how transportation systems evolve. For example, the Williams Street bridge was not included in the modern Dayton rebuild program that occurred from around 2006 to 2019. It was not rebuilt due to the proximity of the Broadway Street

Bridge remnants: in various locations in Dayton, one can see where bridges used to cross over waterways. One of the examples is shown here at the former crossing of Bridge Street over the Wolf Creek. *Author photo.*

bridge to the west and the Edwin C. Moses bridge to the east, as well as declining traffic counts on Williams Street. The Bridge Street bridge, which was a steel truss bridge, was essentially replaced by the Philadelphia Street bridge in 2011, five hundred feet to the east. The abutment over Patterson Boulevard was for a bridge that contained an abandoned rail line. At the time of demolition, it had become a homeless encampment.

RIP RAP ROAD TRUSS BRIDGE

North of the city of Dayton, one can find a seemingly out-of-place large steel truss bridge, now closed to automobile travel. It once had been used as part of the regional bikeway system.

This bridge was a key crossing of Rip Rap Road over the Miami River before the road was relocated about five hundred feet to the east in 2002, off the city's wellfield. The historic bridge was completed in 1924. The former segment of Rip Rap Road leading to it traversed from the Dixie Highway to the Miami Villa community, and remnants of that road leading to this crossing still exist.

The Rip Rap Road bridge in 2020. *Author photo.*

This bridge's tall trusses are characteristic of the Pennsylvania truss configuration, an example of bridges built in the latter part of the truss bridge era. There is extensive latticework on the structure, which is on concrete abutments.

In 1997, the bridge was closed to automobile traffic, as it was determined to be "too deteriorated" for such use. In 2000, Montgomery County approved a $6.3 million plan to build a new bridge over the Great Miami River, which replaced this older bridge, as well as a similar one to the south. The southern bridge was demolished; this bridge, the northern of the two, was not. The project included the construction of a completely new Rip Rap Road to the east of the former version that utilized the older bridge. The historic truss bridge reopened for use in 2001.

This bridge was rehabilitated for non-motorized traffic in 2006.

QUARANTINE HOSPITAL

The Dayton Quarantine Hospital occupied a spot on the hill behind what is now the main exhibit area of Carillon Park from 1887 through 1949. The original hospital was a small frame building built in 1887 to house smallpox patients. This structure was referred to often in its time and after demolition as the "pestilence house" or "pest house." During an epidemic in 1910, a large cement-and-stucco structure replaced the earlier hospital. It was owned and operated by the City of Dayton, under the control of the city's Welfare Department. A news article from 1932 described the site as follows: "The quarantine hospital lies south of Dayton, immediately north of Calvary Cemetery. Leaving a broad sweep of beautiful Patterson Boulevard, the visitor reaches the hospital grounds by a steady climb over a picturesque road, which leads to the institution proper."

This building contained beds for approximately thirty patients. Longtime hospital superintendent Marianne von Greyerz and her family—her husband, Egon, and their six children—lived in the residence portion of the building, which was located on the ground level, below the hospital. Marianne was superintendent from 1923 until the final days of its intended function in 1949. Friends of the von Greyerz children were known to come play in the surrounding woods or play hide-and-seek among the headstones in the adjacent Calvary Cemetery. Marianne oversaw the hospital operations through this time, during which the focus of the hospital changed from

The Quarantine Hospital was originally intended to serve those with smallpox but would later take on other roles. It was demolished in 1949. *Courtesy of Dayton History*.

Remnants of the Quarantine Hospital that operated from 1887 to 1949 on the hill south of today's Carillon Park. *Author photo*.

treating those with smallpox to housing patients in need of treatment for sexually transmitted diseases and alcoholism. There were also blocks of years when the structure received little or no use for its intended purpose, as there were no outbreaks for which this site was needed for treatment.

The superintendent, at least once, laughingly remarked that should widespread vaccination ever be instituted, they would lose their jobs— which is exactly what would eventually occur. The quarantine function was used only one time from 1938 to 1942. The Quarantine Hospital—once a site where victims "died like flies"—closed in 1949, and the property was purchased by Edward Deeds, chairman of the board of National Cash Register, in 1953 for $22,500. He then donated it to Carillon Historical Park.

Throughout the time of the facility, 527 smallpox cases were recorded, with no deaths directly attributed to the disease. From 1943 to 1949, 700 women with venereal disease were treated under the supervision of Nurse von Greyerz. Although the building was demolished in 1955, remnants such as the foundations and steps of the second building can be found in an isolated location on the hill, quietly overlooking the more popular and visible exhibits. Reflecting on the care provided by the von Greyerz family, a retrospective news article in 1995 noted, "The site is now overgrown and scattered with debris. Nothing remains of the caring place for the less fortunate only memories of a family growing up." However, as it often turns out, it is not entirely true that "nothing remains."

AWAITING OLD GLORY

At the former Parkside Homes public housing site, near the corner of Keowee and Helena Streets, in a vast open field, along a no-outlet vacant street (Brennan Drive) sits an old, unadorned flagpole with a surprisingly elaborate base. Not many people see it, given its location, but when you do, it is pretty curious to ponder its presence.

The Parkside Homes development, a $2,250,000 project, was first occupied in 1941. A news article at the time noted, "In the Parkside Homes dwelling the family will enjoy all of the conveniences of a modern home at a cost of $19 a month, including all utilities."

Located in front of what was the administration building of Parkside, the flagpole greeted visitors to this central component of the development. It was located inside a circular drive. It was at this location exactly where,

The Parkside Homes housing development has been demolished, but the flagpole that once greeted visitors still remains. *Author photo*.

on July 22, 1941, as the first residents moved in, music was played by the St. Joseph Orphanage band and Boy Scouts raised a brand-new American flag to the top of the flagpole. Guest speakers spoke optimistically about the future of the development and the need for public housing.

At its peak, Parkside contained over six hundred housing units. It primarily served the white community, while DeSoto Bass in the Miami Chapel neighborhood served the African American community. The Parkside community was demolished in 2008, leaving behind wooded open space. It is a curiosity why the demolition crew left a flagpole behind after the demolition. A gift for urban explorers, perhaps?

THE GHOST STREET

Running southwest from the intersection of Fifth and Keowee Streets is a curious find in an old urban renewal area. The urban renewal project was called East Dayton, the previous neighborhood, Haymarket. And yet, traversing an otherwise open greenspace are the remnants of an old street,

These are the remnants of a street that existed before the urban renewal era. Its path, including the brick surface, is remarkably preserved near the intersection of Keowee and East Fifth Streets. *Author photo.*

Aerial image showing the area of East Fifth Street that would later contain Dayton Towers. *Author photo.*

currently highlighted by solitary seating benches and large trees, as well the brick surface that is being overgrown with ground cover.

This little stretch is filled with history, first through it being a feeder to the Miami Erie Canal and later as a street in the old Haymarket area. The street would go through a series of names over time, most notably Pearl and Haymarket. It ceased to be a proper street around 1960. Today, not only does this path mark that street, but it also is above a large storm drain, undoubtedly located there because of the old canal path. It shares the urban renewal area with Dayton Towers and Jaycee Towers residential buildings. This is an exceptional historical feature because urban renewal projects were notoriously efficient at erasing previous physical features within the project boundaries.

LUNATIC LEGACY

The Southern Ohio Lunatic Asylum is a historic structure at 2335 Wayne Avenue in Dayton. It was constructed in 1855 and added to the National Register of Historic Places in 1979. The complex was constructed as a mental asylum in the design of Philadelphia psychiatrist Thomas Story Kirkbride, in the nationally recognized layout known as the Kirkbride plan. The distinctive main building at the intersection of Wayne and Wilmington Avenues is now an assisted living facility. What many people may not know is how widespread the geographic footprint of influence came to be.

The hospital also had a working farm, in what is now east Kettering, tended by mental patients. The farm is now Kettering's Miami Valley Research Park, and other hospital land is now the site of private homes and Hospice of Dayton.

In 1875, the name was changed to Western Ohio Hospital for the Insane; in 1877, to the Dayton Hospital for the Insane; in 1878, to the Dayton Asylum for the Insane; and in 1894, to the Dayton State Hospital.

The original building contained six wards, three on either side of the administration building, with a capacity of 164. In 1861, the capacity of the hospital was increased to 600 by the addition of six additional wards on each

This building at the corner of Wayne and Wilmington Avenues was constructed in 1855 as the South Ohio Lunatic Asylum. *Courtesy of Dayton History.*

side. In 1891, it was again enlarged by the addition of congregate dining rooms, one on each side, bringing it to a total capacity at this time of 770. In The state property would consist of about three hundred acres.

Much has changed over time. The building was almost demolished. The State of Ohio had to be convinced to postpone for six months the demolition of the main building. The postponement is revealed in a letter from the department to state senator Charles Curran, who requested the delay to give those who wanted to preserve the building time to find a use for it and the funds to purchase, maintain and convert it.

Once a place where some patients were allegedly bound in straightjackets or shackled to walls, it would become abandoned and fall victim to vandals and arsonists who ravaged the Victorian-Italianate-style landmark. The primary, central rooftop dome collapsed during an arson fire that damaged the central section of the building. The building was not in use at the time of the fire, but back in 1894, when the asylum became the Dayton State Hospital for the Insane, it was part of a self-contained community with its power plant and water tower.

The administration building was vacated by the Dayton Mental Health Center in 1978. In 1979, it was listed in the U.S. Interior Department's National Register of Historic Places. The property was deeded by the state to a union foundation in August 1982 and currently serves as an assisted living facility.

Fallout

Two of the very few remaining fallout shelter signs in Dayton are located at the Holden House building at Fifth and Perry Streets and the former school building for Holy Trinity Church at 266 Bainbridge Street. Until recently, such a sign was also located at the Graphics Terminal building at 136 North St. Clair Street. These relics recall a tense time when survival in the case of a nuclear bomb was at the forefront of disaster planning. Fallout shelters were part of a strategic program to designate areas of refuge upon the explosion of a nuclear device.

During the Cold War, many countries built fallout shelters for high-ranking government officials and crucial military facilities. Plans were made, however, to use existing buildings with sturdy below-ground-level basements as makeshift fallout shelters. These buildings were marked with

An outdated sign showing the designation of the building at 200 West Fifth Street as containing a fallout shelter. *Author photo.*

the yellow-and-black trefoil sign designed by the United States Army Corps of Engineers director of administrative logistics support function Robert W. Blakeley in 1961. In September 1961, the federal government started the Community Fallout Shelter Program.

One can certainly understand the desire to establish such sites. In a 1971 news article, it was noted that "Dickson T. Burrows, local Civil Defense director, thinks the entire Dayton metropolitan area would be a likely target in a total war." He says the enemy would aim to destroy "any industrial or production areas in the United States, missile bases, even ordinary cities that have ordinary military and training bases with no real warfare production." Montgomery-Greene County Civil Defense had at that time 571 designated fallout shelters that could accommodate 280,000 of the 700,000 people in the two counties. However, the article notes, if a nuclear bomb or warhead were dropped on Third and Main or Wright-Patterson Air Force Base, even if you had time to run to the nearest shelter, "you are dead." Burrows goes on to state, "The two things they will do with a nuclear attack are, there would definitely be a lot of people killed—that would create the fear of warfare they want—and they'd want to destroy our productivity and input of manpower. If they want to shoot at Dayton, they will hit Dayton. I don't try to kid anybody. I'm not telling people I'm saving lives because I am not. We're simply trying to give people a chance."

The United States ended federal funding for the shelters in the 1970s. Many cities subsequently began removing the iconic signs since members of the public are, of course, unlikely to find viable food and medicine inside those rooms. The signs that still exist today are a reminder of these fearful times.

NEWFIELDS

Because of its location, it is easy to dismiss this development as a rather traditional, perhaps stalled, suburban housing project that coincidentally is situated near a state park. But something was planned and then did not happen. Something that was created by an ambitious strategy. Ambitions to contain forty thousand residents. And that state park? That state park (Sycamore State Park) was established where many of those residents were planned to be located. This is the story of Newfields.

The development of Newfields emerged from the Federal New Communities program, which was established in 1970. This program was intended to establish new, planned areas of development and was to be carried out by the U.S. Department of Housing and Urban Development (HUD), in partnership with a private corporation.

Planning for Newfields began in 1973. One of the key components to the development, which was different than other suburbs at the time, was the installation of a "community authority" that would be able to not only oversee programs and improvements but also be able to collect an income assessment for such considerations. The authority was given wide breadth of responsibility, including overseeing parks, community facilities, daycare, volunteer programs and social services.

Concerns over the four-thousand-acre development envisioned to accommodate forty thousand residents emerged quickly, including impact on local schools and transportation systems, although the transportation concerns were to be mitigated by the eventual construction of U.S. 35 and what was then referred to as I-675 West, which would become a rerouted OH 49.

Initial road construction began later in 1973, with the construction of Newfields Boulevard and Brookston Road, in what used to be a soybean field in Madison Township.

One of the few buildings that were actually constructed at the Newfields site. It was to be part of the village community center. *Author photo.*

The vast peaceful area that was once to contain a new city. *Author photo.*

While Newfields was established under the New Towns program, it was never going to be any kind of independent, autonomous jurisdiction. The four-thousand-acre site was, from early inception, divided up among Trotwood, Dayton and unincorporated Montgomery County. A formula for annexation was drafted, with the rest to be unincorporated. Even a successful development would be little more than a large subdivision or neighborhood. The community president at the time likened the Newfields identity to a neighborhood "like Dayton View, or some other area of Dayton."

Newfields developers pressed on, however, and in 1974, a commercial building was completed, with design by famed Victor Gruen and Associates with local input from architect Richard Levin. At this point, there was still reason for optimism.

The cracks in the plan started to show in 1976. Disagreement arose between the developer, Donald Huber, and the HUD. Huber was having trouble receiving the money he felt should have been flowing from HUD, citing regulatory barriers and what was alleged as a personal grudge between Huber and a HUD official. Ultimately, HUD had lost confidence in the project. Around this time, there were a handful of housing units already built, and it was starting to become clear Newfields was heading in the wrong direction.

A major obstacle was the political fragmentation of the site. There was extensive discussion over who could or would annex the Newfields property, especially after Huber defaulted on federally backed bonds for the community. A salvage plan emerged where HUD would retain 1,525 acres of the development and find a developer to replace the ousted Huber. Much of the land that Dayton was supposed to annex was to be included in the new state park. The park was to be located on about 2,000 acres in the west and central portions of the project, with the Ohio Department of Natural Resources willing to spend $4 million to purchase the land, which would be bought from Montgomery County after the City of Dayton backed out of the deal.

The residential development would ultimately stall, uncompleted. The initial buildings would remain, and the state park development was implemented. Several retrospectives on what went wrong would follow in years to come, including a 1979 article in the *Cincinnati Enquirer* titled "Newfields's $21 Million Death," referring to the governmental cost of the failed community. The development was started in a time of economic depression with promises of federal money for public facilities and low- and middle-income housing. Then, the money never really came, and the money that did arrive was late to the development. There was an almost immediate cash flow problem to pay off the debt that had been backed by HUD. Additionally, vast political change occurred at this time, each step being one step further away from the original vision of the development. The 1979 article concludes, "It began as Utopia and is ending as one of 13 national headaches."

The Newfields project site today is an eerily quiet landscape dotted by unused infrastructure, such as bike paths, parking lots and public spaces. But there is no significant public to fill such spaces, no cars to fill the parking lots.

THE LEGACY OF DR. SHAWEN

Odlin Woods is an approximately thirty-acre tree-filled area in the north part of Dayton, along Odlin Avenue, just south of Siebenthaler Avenue. One might see it and wonder why such a large wooded tract would exist in an urban area. Why has this land never been developed, like the rest of the land around it?

Its history is as an old estate, that of Peter Odlin, originally. Peter Odlin, a prominent lawyer, sold the property, including the estate home at 401 Odlin Avenue, to the Shawen family shortly before World War I. Dr. Charles Shawen would live there until 1951. He was previously a physician and surgeon for twenty-five years until he retired in 1929. He was a past chief of staff at Miami Valley Hospital. His wife, Agnes, died in a fire at the home in 1956. Mrs. Shawen was found on the second-floor sun porch that traversed the front of the house. It was noted that fire suppression efforts were hindered by the many trees and other vegetation on the property. There appears to be no remaining trace of the house, but the wooded area remains, now in the ownership of the City of Dayton.

In 1949, it was noted that the Shawen/Odlin property had become a bird sanctuary, hosting a roost of an estimated one hundred thousand birds in the relatively small area. Dr. Shawen had posted the area as a refuge in which not hunting was not permitted. Dr. Shawen was well known for his gardening. At the rear of the Odlin home, in the "farm-within-the-city" was allegedly the largest gladiolus bed in the state—at one time it was reported that there were 1,800 different varieties of gladiolus growing there.

This isn't the only major legacy of Dr. Shawen in this area or even this part of the city. In 1926, he donated nineteen acres for a children's home,

The only remaining cottage of the former Shawen Acres children's home. *Author photo.*

with a deed restriction that the property would always be used to house "homeless children." He and his brother Thomas Shawen gave the land for the children's home on North Main Street in 1926 as a memorial to their parents, Mr. and Mrs. Edward L. Shawen, and their two sons, Charles E. Jr. and Robert. This would become Shawen Acres, located at 3304 North Main Street. At one time, this property contained ten English-style children's cottages and an administrative building, with up to three hundred children living on the campus. In 2013, nine of the cottages were demolished after years of neglect and damage. One cottage, the only one-story version, remains on the site. Two picnic shelters were constructed using materials salvaged from the demolished structures. A walking path was installed in place of the demolished cottages. The property is owned by Montgomery County and is home to the Haines Children's Center.

THE SHORTEST HIGHWAY

The Hamilton-Wyoming Connector, built to controlled-access highway standards, opened in October 1971. It was subsequently renamed Steve

Whalen Boulevard on March 11, 1992, which generally coincided with the thoroughfare being transformed from a highway to a boulevard, although in reality, the highway-like appearance persists to this day.

To those who are not familiar with the background on Steve Whalen Boulevard, its very existence is puzzling. It was born out of an attempt to create a highway system around and through the eastern part of the city of Dayton, cutting through densely building neighborhoods—an inner beltway of sorts. Opposition from residents and limited funding ultimately stopped the highway project. Therefore, the Steve Whalen stretch—at a distance of 0.72 miles—is a short, isolated segment of highway connecting Wyoming Street and Hamilton Avenue.

The course of the envisioned highway would have connected Stanley Avenue to Wilmington Avenue while going right through the Walnut Hills neighborhood and the state mental institute property at Wayne and Wilmington Avenues. While Steve Whalen Boulevard and its overbuilt section are an absurd out-of-context outlier, that the project was stopped was likely a very good thing for Dayton neighborhoods.

The connector is part of an inner belt plan first proposed in 1952, with the objective to carry traffic around the central business district via a route that would include Stanley Avenue on the north, Highland Avenue on the East,

Steve Whalen Boulevard, once planned to be a segment on an urban "innerbelt," now is an isolated remnant of that vision. *Author photo.*

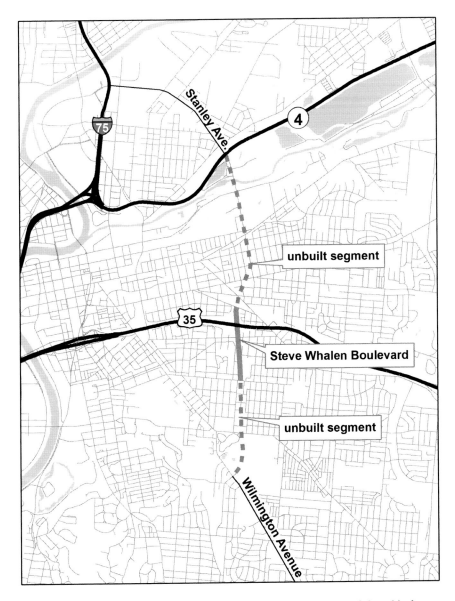

The proposed Stanley-Wilmington Connector. This is the proposed route of the vehicular artery. Ultimately, only the path from Hamilton to Wyoming was constructed. *Map by author.*

Stewart Street on the South, and Broadway Street to the west. In fact, some moderate improvements did occur on these streets, but the real highway development was yet to come. In 1968, the eastern project was included in a thoroughfare plan presented to the city Plan Board as the "Stanley-

Wilmington Connector." Opposition mobilized quickly. By 1970, a headline observed, "Connector Plan Dies in E. Dayton Meeting," noting that "more than 399 East Dayton residents attended funeral services Thursday night for the Stanley-Wilmington connector. Apparently, all that remains is for city commission to bury the body."

The City Commission did exactly that, in response to neighborhood opposition in Walnut Hills and Ohmer Park, but not soon enough to stop the Hamilton to Wyoming section.

The Stanley-Wilmington Connector became the Hamilton-Wyoming Connector. Fears were prevalent that this would cause massive traffic problems in adjacent neighborhoods, which never really materialized. Even in 1970—before the highway section was built—there was discussion regarding changes that should be made to "tame" the highway stretch.

It was an unceremonious epitaph upon opening in 1971. A headline declared, "$7 Million Dead End Opens in East Dayton." The article goes on to suggest, "It has to be a candidate for the distinct position of being this nation's tiniest, costliest and most controversial expressways." A nearby resident added that the highway is the "silliest darn thing I ever heard of."

In 1974, the larger project, from Stanley to Wilmington, was officially removed from the city's thoroughfare plan.

BRICK STREETS

Brick streets are beloved relics of the past. Brick, attractive and utilitarian in the present day, was the first durable street surface. The first concrete street in Dayton was Virginia Avenue, which was installed in 1914. And while bricks still underlay many asphalt streets in older areas of the city, some have yet to be covered with such, or in other cases, the asphalt has been removed to redisplay the brick surface. Brick was the common street surface of its time. It provided, generally, a long-lasting, durable travel surface. The city of Dayton has approximately nine miles of roadway with a brick surface, including prominent streets like East Fifth Street through the Oregon District and Williams Street in Wright Dunbar, as well as not-so-well-known streets, such as Indianola Avenue in North Riverdale and Milburn Avenue in McCook Field. The newest brick-surfaced street in the inventory is Dutoit Street in St. Anne's Hill.

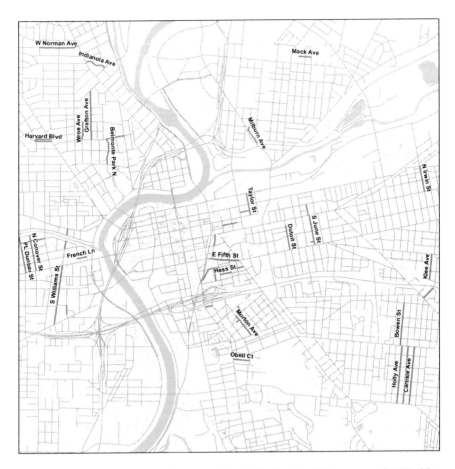

This map shows the brick streets that currently exist in the city of Dayton, as of 2020. *Map by author.*

As it was about to be resurfaced with asphalt in 2018, it was decided by residents that the brick surface was preferred. Similarly, many of the brick streets in the Oregon District were daylighted through the work of the residents of the neighborhood.

Urban Grain Silos

One does not expect to see grain silos in the heart of an urban area. Yet Dayton has a large set in its rapidly redeveloping Webster Station neighborhood, just

These grain silos at the southeast corner of East Third and Meigs Streets, once part of the Vitality Feed Mills Company, are a unique sight in the middle of an urban area. *Author photo.*

to the northeast of the downtown core. These silos were constructed along the B&O Railroad line, to the southwest of the intersection of First and Keowee Streets at 16 Meigs Street. The silos were used by a company called Vitality Feed Mills.

Vitality Mills, based in Chicago, purchased the property on Meigs Street in 1945. It was an ideal location, with easy access to the highways of the time, including Routes 4, 35, 48, 49, 25, 201 and 202, and of course the adjacent rail line. The plant was completely renovated and the company was in growth mode, with two other mills, both in Illinois. It was noted as being an essential industry for national defense, claiming to be the "sixth most essential industry for the war effort." "A supply of quality feeds for poultry and livestock for feed dealers will definitely be an immediate aid for greater meat and egg production," the company said. The company produced feed for chickens, turkeys, cows, horses, hogs, goats, pigeons, rabbits and dogs. The company was twenty-six years old at the time, with many dealers throughout the region. In moving to the site, Vitality bought it from the V.E. Herter Company, then one of the oldest feed companies in Dayton, having been at the site since 1912. The Herter Company provided grain market reports on prices delivered to the grain elevator to the newspapers in its years at the

Meigs location. At the time, the capacity of the mill and grain elevators was sixteen thousand bushels, including a warehouse that was constructed at the site in 1927 at a cost of $22,000. The structure was two stories in height and of reinforced concrete. It was at 26–28 Meigs Street.

After Vitality left the site, it was owned by N.O. Nelson, which sold appliances. Since then, N.O. Nelson morphed into a company called Winnelson, one of the nation's largest plumbing supply distributors, and is now part of the Winsupply family of companies, based in Moraine.

Today, the silos are vacant but certainly represent an opportunity for a unique adaptive reuse. Until then, their mere existence is an exceptional monument to the past.

Lost Art

The year was 1989, and Dayton was trying to express itself as progressive in the public art arena. Commissions were prevalent around this time, and one of the pieces that drew substantial interest was *Street Link*. *Street Link* was designed by New York artist Andrea Blum. Blum received a commission of $10,000 for her work, which would ultimately cost $61,000 in total.

The piece was a concrete podium with a steel railing. It offers the practical purpose of visually connecting the west side of Dayton to the Great Miami River and downtown Dayton. The concrete was colored yellow and green.

The piece was not universally lauded upon installation, including a public official calling it "a monument to committees." It was paid for by the Miami Valley Arts Council and public funds.

What does the site look like today? Well, it's easy to see it and not so easy to see it as public art. Some think it is a foundation of a long-demolished building or one that never quite got built. The colored concrete has faded, and grass has taken over. But if allowed, the concrete will remain for many years—an isolated concrete formation, a relic of an ambitious art program. "If people spent more time looking at something without trying to identify it, then you've allowed the experience to enter your life," said Blum. While the art may not endure, the sentiment behind this quote certainly does.

Other public art or public history pieces dot the western side of the river as well. These include a non-operating fountain dedicated to the memory of Adam Schantz (a prolific Dayton builder of the early twentieth century); a memorial evergreen tree, dedicated with a plaque, planted for a loved one

The public art piece *Street Link* is part of a series of interesting features along the western edge of the Dayton riverfront. *Author photo.*

in 1974; a flagpole donated to the City of Dayton by the American Legion in 1924; a seating bench dedicated to a former Dayton city commissioner; a stone wall that was part of the area where the Private Fair statue once stood (it is now located on Main Street at Monument Avenue); and Holbrooke Plaza, named for Richard Holbrooke, who led the Dayton Peace Accords in 1995. Holbrooke Plaza features masonry elements from historic structures in Bosnia and Herzegovina.

RIVER'S EDGE PARK

Intended to be an integral part of the Dayton riverfront, River's Edge Park represents a relatively large investment, ultimately unfulfilled. It is located just north of the Landing apartments, on the south bank of the Great Miami River. It includes large concrete forms and steps and a couple of recognition signs. The site was developed as part of the river corridor plan in the 1980s. It did have a noticeable short prime as a destination and gathering place of sorts but has been relatively ignored in recent decades.

The plan was announced in 1978 by River Corridor park planners, who wanted an amphitheater at the low dam at this location. The plans included a permanent, "hull-shaped" concrete stage and viewing areas. The viewing area was provided by a large set of concrete steps that could accommodate up to one thousand patrons. This would all complement the large pool of water created by the low dam, which was under construction at the time and was to provide a popular use as a recreation destination. It was described as "a 1.4-mile-long pool for boating." There was also supposed to be something called a floating fountain. The architects of the project were Lorenz and Williams. Work began in 1979 and was completed in 1980, with the first full season a heavily programmed 1981 season.

It was not long before the site, River's Edge Park, became a $1.3 million relic. A 1996 news article titled "The Park Nobody Wants to Use" noted the following: "The amphitheater at River's Edge park won three major architectural awards when it was built behind the YMCA in 1980....So the park stands forbiddingly deserted, stained by graffiti, with trash washing up on its banks."

Today, it is a true relic. It is overlooked and mostly unmaintained, in a relatively ruinous state, although it still has a bit of a sculptural appearance. It would seem that it will one day be rehabbed or replaced as the city continues to focus attention on the riverfront.

The remains of River's Edge Park on the south bank of the Great Miami River. It is a solitary experience, as the site has not been programmed in many years. *Author photo.*

HONORARY DESIGNATIONS

A relatively simple way of incrementally recognizing significant Dayton figures has evolved into a bit of a glossary of these geographic recognitions. An honorary designation is the installation of the blue (in Dayton) street signs that recognize various characters of significance. They are established as an ordinance by the Dayton City Commission. Many are approved as two-year designations, and then, after the two years, the signs typically remain. The following are the honorary designations in the city of Dayton.

- Ambassador Richard Holbrooke Memorial Bridge—Salem Avenue Bridge: Richard Holbrook (1941–2010) was an American diplomat. Most relevant to Dayton, he was a leader in the development of the Dayton Accords in 1995, which brought an end to the Bosnian war.

- Avenue of the Arts—Main Street: Designated as such due to the arts destinations in the vicinity.

- Betsy B. Whitney Way—Wilkinson Street: Named in honor of Betsy Whitney for her extensive volunteer and philanthropic efforts, including those toward the YWCA, which is located on Wilkinson Street.

- Bishop John H. Mathews Jr. Way—College Street: John H. Mathews was pastor of Mount Zion Church.

- Chuck Whalen Lane—L Street: Chuck Whalen (1920–2011) was a University of Dayton graduate who would go on to serve as a U.S. representative.

- Commissioner Richard A. Zimmer Memorial Bridge—Findlay Street Bridge: Richard Zimmer was a Dayton City commissioner for twenty-one years.

- Dean Lovelace Drive—Madden Hills: Dean Lovelace was a Dayton city commissioner.

- Dr. Martin Luther King Jr. Way—Third Street: The primary surface street connecting the east and west sides of the city is a fitting one for this designation.

- Erma Bombeck Way—Brown and Warren Streets: Erma Bombeck (1927–1996) was a writer whose popular humor column was widely read nationally. She grew up in Dayton.

- Keith A. Byers Sr. Way—Hoover Avenue: Keith Byers is a Dayton native who played in the National Football League for thirteen seasons.

- Lloyd Lewis Jr. Way—Ludlow Street: Lloyd Lewis Jr. was a city of Dayton assistant city Manager, city commissioner, state representative, an executive at Rike's department store and vice president at Dayton Power & Light.

- Local 696 Way—Alwildy Drive: United Auto Workers Local 696 has a headquarters building on Alwildy Drive, which was designed by Paul Deneau in 1965.

- Martin Bayless Drive—Enroe Drive: Martin Bayless is a Dayton native who played in the National Football League for thirteen seasons.

- Mick Montgomery Way—Patterson Boulevard: Mick Montgomery owned Canal Street Tavern, a music venue in downtown Dayton.

- Mike Schmidt Parkway—Riverside Drive: Mike Schmidt, a Dayton native, played in Major League Baseball for eighteen seasons, where he was three-time Most Valuable Player and twelve-time All-Star. He was inducted into the Hall of Fame in 1995.

- Page E. Gray Jr. Way—Liscum Drive: Page E. Gray was the first African American to hold a position other than custodian at the National Cash Register Company. He was a parts inspector and later an assistant design engineer during the 1960s.

Fourth Street in downtown, adjacent to the Grant-Deneau Tower, has an honorary designation for architect Paul Deneau. *Author photo.*

- Pastor S.N. Winston Sr. Way—Siebenthaler Road: Samuel N. Winston Sr. was a pastor at Mount Calvary Missionary Baptist Church for forty-six years.

- Paul Deneau Way—Fourth Street: Paul Deneau was an architect of several significant Dayton buildings, including the Grant-Deneau Tower at 40 West Fourth Street and the Lakewoods Tower at 980 Wilmington Avenue.

- Peace Bridge—Third Street Bridge: This bridge connects two sides of the Great Miami River.

- Richard A. Zimmer Memorial Bridge—Findlay Street Bridge: Richard A. Zimmer was a Dayton city commissioner for over twenty-one years.

- Sergeant Edward Brooks Way—Elmhurst Drive: Edward Brooks was killed at age twenty-five by an improvised explosive device on August 29, 2007, in Ramadi, Iraq, while serving during Operation Iraqi Freedom.

- Ted Mills Way—Sears Street: Ted Mills is recognized due to his contributions to amateur baseball. He has a baseball school location on Sears Street.

- Walter J. Hickman Sr. Avenue—Brooklyn Avenue: Walter Hickman Sr. was a respected neighborhood leader in the Westwood area, in which Brooklyn Avenue is located.

- Willis "Bing" Davis Way—Diamond Avenue: Bing Davis is a locally and nationally renowned artist who grew up on Diamond Avenue.

- Wright Brothers Parkway—Turner Road, Shoup Mill Road, Needmore Road, Harshman Road, Woodman Drive: Dayton's most famous locals are honored with a series of connecting streets that loop around the city and its inner-ring suburbs.

CHAPTER 8

SUBTERRANEAN DAYTON

The underground of any city is both an active place and a deserted place. Strictly utilitarian, yet complex. The underground of Dayton seems to have a particular formative impact, playing a role in the industrial ascent of the region. Large industrial companies often used underground passages to get from building to building. Dayton was an early adopter of steam technology and maintained it for much longer than others. All of this, of course, is in addition to the geologic bounty of the Great Miami Buried Aquifer and the Dayton limestone formation.

Two of the most important companies in Dayton's history used tunnels to traverse their numerous industrial buildings—the National Cash Register (NCR) Company and the Delco Products Division or Delco/Frigidaire.

The NCR tunnel system connected many of the various NCR buildings, including Building 26. One of the doors of the tunnel system is located at Carillon Park. An entrance into the now blocked and collapsed system still exists about 850 feet southwest of the intersection of River Corridor Drive and South Main Street. It was through these tunnels that workers and materials moved, as "The Cash" emerged as an industrial giant. One certainly imagines the importance of the tunnels during World War II, when Daytonian Joe Desch, under tremendous pressure, worked to solve the German Enigma. For this and many other endeavors, the tunnels brought great utility. Today, the tunnels are sometimes encountered upon new construction in the area. According to Ken Carr, a former NCR employee, "There were nine main tunnels spanning nearly one-half mile in length." It

A passageway that once led to the National Cash Register tunnel system, which connected the buildings of the campus. *Author photo.*

is reported that small electric trucks commonly traversed the tunnels, which were approximately 8 feet high by 8 feet wide. These "baby electric trucks" were reportedly actually made by the National Cash Register Company. Over time, the importance of these trucks, often modified to suit a specific purpose, would expand and carry out many different transport and delivery services throughout the NCR campus.

Another historic Dayton company to utilize an underground tunnel system connecting multiple buildings is Delco/Frigidaire or Delco Products Division. One of the more well known of these is the one under First Street connecting 329 East First Street (Plant 1) to 340 East First Street (Plant 2). The plants were used for the manufacturing of electric motors and generators. This was a pair of tunnels that also carried utilities, including steam, between the two properties. The presence of the two tunnels enabled for better structural support and, of course, easier passing. News reports of the time marveled at not just the tunnel but especially that the construction of a large passage under a street while navigating and relocating utilities was done with only minor closures and inconvenience, noting, "The construction of the tunnel, which required extraordinary skill, was accomplished without causing great inconvenience to anyone, despite the fact that streetcar traffic had to be cared for while the work was in progress." The tunnel also encountered a large sanitary sewer main and power lines, as well as storm sewer, water and natural and artificial gas pipes. The roof is supported by steel beams, which also carried utilities. One of the primary benefits of the tunnel was that those traversing between the two buildings would no longer have to cross streetcar tracks. The cost was approximately $12,000. Another tunnel led from 329 East First Street to a now demolished Delco building where the minor-league baseball stadium now stands. There is an even lesser-known tunnel that connects the two sides of the rail line at a location north of East First Street, just to the west of Keowee Street. That tunnel partially remains today, although it is closed off. All of the buildings in that area have been demolished, leaving the tunnel behind.

If underground activity played a role in two of Dayton's most prominent companies, it also played a prominent role in what is probably Dayton's most prominent building: the Dayton Arcade. The subterranean role was essential; it was here where it served as an underground cold storage area, which is important because the Arcade was a marketplace from its beginning. The ability to use this area for such meant that perishable foods could stay fresh longer, and the Arcade could serve as the commercial hub it was intended to be. The market stalls relied on the twelve-thousand-square-foot underground cold storage area. The basement featured the power plant for the building, the cold storage plant and machinery for the elevators. The power plant was built for $125,000 and provided electricity to the various buildings. It was located beneath the Ludlow Street building. The cold storage refrigeration was also provided to each of the market stalls. The building also utilized the downtown steam system and was designed so that all produce would be taken by wagon into the basement and from there distributed to the stalls above, avoiding the clutter that arose at other market areas.

The Dayton VA has an underground history that spans underground tunnels for utilities and for transport—both by the living and of the deceased. They were referred to as the "Great Underground Avenues." They were originally primarily intended as passageways for utilities under the VA grounds. The tunnels were six feet high and seven feet wide and located at a depth of six feet below the surface. Reports from an 1885 article in the *Dayton Herald* talk about the massive scale of the tunnel work. Ultimately, though, the tunnels evolved to serve the role of transport. "These underground avenues are large enough for men to walk in them, and are roomy enough to permit five or six walking abreast," the 1885 article noted.

One of the VA tunnels is currently a target for preservation. In the early 1990s, Mark Kucharski was directed to oversee a scope of work that included the removal of one particular tunnel. He determined that it should not go forward due to the tunnel's history. This tunnel was said to be built in the 1870s and led from the site of the former hospital building to what is now the Dayton National Cemetery. The entrance was constructed of limestone, presumably Dayton Formation. After leaving the tunnel, the body would be taken by horse-drawn carriage to the grave site. This tunnel is larger than the other VA tunnels; it measures seven feet in height and eight feet wide. About fifty feet of the original three-hundred-foot-long passage is still intact. The peak number of deaths was around 1,400 annually toward the end of the nineteenth century. The hospital from which the bodies were taken from burned down in 1942, but the funeral tunnel was left in place. An article in the *Dayton Daily News* described the usage of the tunnel as follows: "For a funeral procession from the tunnel, a body was transported to the tunnel in a casket and placed on a small flat car and moved through the underground passage, according to Ball State. The funeral corps would then place the casket into the waiting horse-drawn hearse and a line of forty or more soldiers would form outside the tunnel entrance." Recently, a group of researchers from Ball State University provided those three options and analyzed the condition of the tunnel, which was found to be surprisingly good. Now, three options have been developed for preservation. One would include the reconstruction of the façade, including a new limestone entrance, the steps and an iron gate. These items were features of the original but are now in various states of deterioration. A second option would restore the entrance, as well as a portion of the tunnel. Finally, a third option is to restore the entire tunnel, including the receiving vault.

Another pedestrian tunnel connected the north end of Bainbridge Street to East Third Street, tunneling under a railroad bridge. This former pedestrian connection is truly hidden. You probably would not notice it if you were not looking for it; even if you were, it is very difficult to find. It is covered by a blocked-in cement block wall bounded to the south by loads of fill. What existed here was a pedestrian connection between Bainbridge Street and Third Street, connecting the Dayton Motor Car historic district to the DPL Historic District, both of which are listed in the National Register of Historic Places. The northern end of the tunnel leads to Third Street, just to the east of where Third Street and Webster Street intersect. The southern end of the tunnel comes out on Bainbridge Street. The pedestrian tunnel at Third and Bainbridge Streets was about 115 feet long, about 10 feet wide and 10 feet high. One wonders if it can one day be returned to its previous

This tunnel entrance at the Dayton VA could be reopened someday. *Author photo.*

Obstructed entrance to the partially underground tunnel that connected Bainbridge and East Third Streets. *Author photo.*

usage. It certainly seems like it could provide a useful connection, if not now, then as the area continues to redevelop.

The underground area could also provide useful cover for leisure activities, such as for speakeasies in the time of Prohibition. One of those that recently "surfaced" is in the basement of the building at 108–24 East Third Street, between St. Clair and Jefferson Streets. It was at this location where a bottle emblazed with the name "Belle of Dayton" was found during a construction project in the building. The 124 East Third Street building was built in 1919—the same year the Volstead Act brought Prohibition. Among the evidence is the finishes and materials of the basement space. To have such a high-quality level of finish does not seem to make sense for a regular secluded basement backroom. It is in great contrast with the rest of the plain concrete basement. It is an eighty-by-twenty-foot room with a raised wood plank floor, ornate plaster moldings on silver-painted walls and the remnants of wiring for ceiling lighting. And the path to it draws interest. At one time, there was direct access from the outside to this relatively decorative basement room. It is said that one could enter the building from a (now long torn-down) carriage shack and through a rear door. A winding hallway led to the supposed drinking establishment.

One of the more unique underground features in Dayton is the former downtown steam system. Underground steam connections helped make Dayton an industrial powerhouse. The first underground steam lines were constructed in 1907, serving nineteen customers. Steam was conceived as a heat source because it was a byproduct of electrical generation, created from the exhaust of burning coal. The earliest lines were primarily those around the Dayton Arcade, such as Fourth, Ludlow and Third Streets. Steam stations were located near the center of the city, including the now demolished steam plant at Longworth, a station that was constructed in 1929. It could produce two hundred thousand pounds of steam per hour. This was the second steam plant serving downtown; the first was at a building that still exists, fittingly, where the Steam Plant event center is today, at the northwest corner of West Third and Webster Streets. Over time, the system would amount to about nineteen miles of pipe, serving several hundred downtown locations. Both of the stations were originally powered by the burning of coal. However, environmental concerns in the early 1970s caused the Third Street station to be converted to a natural gas–burning facility, while the Longworth station was enhanced with cleaning technology but still burned coal on two boilers, while the other two were converted to fuel oil. From this location, steam was piped through parts of downtown. It was not until 1996 that steam was

This building at 617 East Third Street operated as one of downtown's two steam plants. *Author photo.*

abandoned as a viable electric or heating source. Even today, that connection is relevant because many downtown sidewalks have vaults below them. More recently, these areas have been adapted for new uses, as the Dayton Arcade will use them for transporting material items from street level to the underground. At that time, the steam was coming exclusively from the Steam Plant at East Third and Webster Streets. Discussions continued late into this decision process about the expansion of the steam system regionally, and studies were conducted regarding the feasibility thereof. It was thought that perhaps such a system would cushion the blow of then rapidly rising energy costs. In 1975, a *Dayton Daily News* article said, "Some Dayton Power and Light Co. customers do not worry about soaring electricity rates and shortages of natural gas. They are the 432 customers who buy two billion pounds of water radiant heat—old fashioned steam—each year from DPL." It was reported at that time that Dayton's underground steam heating system ranked thirteenth in size among such systems in the country.

EPILOGUE

I wrote this book sure of one thing—the items discussed herein will not last forever. Certainly, some of them may not be around for much longer at all. Our historic inventory is always evolving. Appreciation for new sites, new time periods, new people emerges over time. Likewise, inevitably, things are demolished and discarded. History churns.

I also know this is far from a comprehensive scope. It represents little more than a sampling and a snapshot. That's the way it has to be, because even if we limit a history to the most hidden variety, it seems—and it certainly seemed writing this book—that one could go on forever. I accept that there are some things I have not included. I do hope that I have increased your appreciation for hidden history, and maybe others can tell me about interesting stories that would have been perfect for this book. In fact, I have no doubt that will occur.

This book has given me an appreciation for the texturized nature of any street, district or neighborhood. Nothing is as it seems—especially in Dayton, but probably anywhere. My favorite topics in this book, in retrospect, are those that I at one time questioned their worthiness, with two examples being the midcentury architecture and a simple flagpole at the former Parkside Homes site. As for the buildings, historic preservation only now appreciates midcentury contributions. Even in Dayton, the buildings of this period were previously seen as the stuff between the historic structures. Appreciating them for their own contribution to the Dayton story alters one's perspective. As for the flagpole, to me, it shows the simplicity of what can make a place interesting. A simple flagpole can provoke interest and a desire to delve into a more revealing story.

I will be happy if this book causes one to see more of the details, to think about why things are how they are, how they got there and what they mean. The urban landscape is the composite of many stories.

I wish you well in discovering the most hidden of these stories. Please do tell me about them.

BIBLIOGRAPHY

Chapter 1

Camp, Mark J. *Roadside Geology of Ohio*. Missoula, MT: Mountain Press Publishing Company, 2006.

Centerville-Washington History. "August F. Foerste." www.centervillewashingtonhistory.org.

Dalton, Curt. *Dayton Through Time*. Charleston, SC: Arcadia Publishing, 2015.

Drury, A.W. *History of the City of Dayton and Montgomery County, Ohio*. Chicago: S.J. Clarke, 1909.

Foerste, August F. "Geology of Dayton and Vicinity." 1915. www.daytonhistorybooks.com/page/page/3836559.htm.

Goldthwait, Richard P. "Scenes in Ohio during the Last Ice Age." *Ohio Journal of Science* 59, no. 4 (July 1959).

Hansen, Michael C. "Geology of Ohio—The Silurian." *Ohio Geology* (Spring 1998). Ohio Department of Natural Resources. academic.udayton.edu/michaelsandy/silurian%20-%20ohiogs%20-%20complete%20silurian%20article.htm.

———. "The Last Ice Age in Ohio." Educational Leaflet No. 7, Revised Edition, 2017 Division of Geological Survey. Ohio Department of Natural Resources. geosurvey.ohiodnr.gov/portals/geosurvey/PDFs/Education/el07.pdf.

Nerny, Nancy, with Sue Williams. "A Visit to Woodland Cemetery and Arboretum, Educator's Guidebook." The Woodland Arboretum Foundation. www.woodlandcemetery.org/images/WLA-Educator-Guidebook.pdf.

Norris, Stanley E., and Andrew M. Spieker. "Ground-water Resources of the Dayton Area, Ohio. Geological Water Supply." Paper 1808. Washington, D.C.: United States Printing Office, 1966.

Ohio Department of Natural Resources. "Glacial Map of Ohio." geosurvey. ohiodnr.gov/portals/geosurvey/pdfs/glacial/glacial.pdf.

———. "Ohio Historical Marker Dedicated at McDonald Quarry, Greene County." Summer 1996. https://geosurvey.ohiodnr.gov/portals/geosurvey/PDFs/Newsletter/Summer96.pdf.

Ohio EPA. "Major Aquifers in Ohio and Associated Water Quality." Division of Drinking and Ground Waters Technical Series on Ground Water Quality, April 2014.

Ray, Louis L. "Geomorphology and Quaternary Geology of the Glaciated Ohio River Valley—A Reconnaissance Study." Geological Survey Paper 826. U.S. Department of Interior. Washington, D.C.: United States Government Printing Office, 1974.

Sandy, Michael D. "The Dayton Limestone." academic.udayton.edu/michaelsandy/DAYTON%20LIMESTONE%20NEW.htm.

———. "Geologic Glimpses from Around the World—The Geology of Monuments in Woodland Cemetery and Arboretum, Dayton, Ohio: A self-Guided Tour." Ohio Department of Natural Resources, 1992.

———. "Our Geology." www.centervillewashingtonhistory.org/historical-events/our-geology.

Schumacher, Gregory A., Michael P. Angle, Brian E. Mott and Douglas J. Aden. "Geology of the Dayton Region in Core and Outcrop—A Workshop and Field Trip for Citizens, Environmental Investigators, Geologists and Educators." Prepared for the 2012 Geological Society of America North Central Section meeting in Dayton, Ohio. Columbus, OH, 2012.

Steele, Robert Wilbur, and Mary Davies Steele. *Early Dayton: With Important Facts and Incidents from the Founding of the City of Dayton, Ohio to the Hundredth Anniversary 1796–1896*. Dayton, OH: U.B. Publishing House, W.J. Shuey, Publisher, 1896.

Wall text. History on the Hill Interpretive Center. "Glacial Remnents." Carillon Park, Dayton, OH.

Chapter 2

Cartaino, Carol. *It Happened in Ohio: Remarkable Events that Shaped History.* Guilford, CT: Morris Book Publishing LLC, 2010.

Curwen, Maskell E. *A Sketch of the History of the City of Dayton.* Dayton, OH: J. Odell Jr., 1850.

Dayton Metro Library. Dayton, Ohio. content.daytonmetrolibrary.org/ digital/api/collection/finding/id/3009/download.

Encyclopedia Britannica. "Aaron Burr." www.britannica.com/biography/ Aaron-Burr#ref173542.

Gelbert, Doug. *Look Up Dayton! Walking Tour of Dayton.* E-book. N.d.

Honious, Ann. *What Dreams We Have: The Wright Brothers and Their Hometown of Dayton, Ohio.* Fort Washington, PA: Eastern National, 2003.

Linklater, Andro. *An Artist in Treason: The Extraordinary Double Life of General James Wilkinson.* New York: Walker and Co., 2009.

NPR. "The Man Who Double-Crossed the Founders." April 28, 2010. www.npr.org/2010/04/28/126363998/the-man-who-double-crossed-the-founders.

Rickey, Lisa, and Jared Balwin. "Finding Aid for the Van Cleve–Dover Special Collection." April 2010. Dayton Metro Library, Dayton, OH.

Ronald, Virgina, and Bruce Ronald. *The Lands Between the Miamis: A Bicentennial Celebration of the Dayton Area.* Dayton, OH: Landfall Press, Inc., 1996.

Steele, Robert Wilbur, and Mary Davies Steele. *Early Dayton: With Important Facts and Incidents from the Founding of the City of Dayton, Ohio to the Hundredth Anniversary 1796–1896.* Dayton, OH: U.B. Publishing House, W.J. Shuey, Publisher, 1896.

Chapter 3

Chanchani, Samiran. Pylon Exhibits, Patterson Boulevard, Dayton, OH.

Downtown Dayton, National Register of Historic Places Nomination. Form preparer, Samiran Chanchani. 2019.

Honious, Ann. *What Dreams We Have: The Wright Brothers and Their Hometown of Dayton, Ohio.* Fort Washington, PA: Eastern National, 2003.

Oeters, Bill, and Nancy Gulick. *Miami and Erie Canal.* Charleston, SC: Arcadia Publishing, 2014.

Chapter 4

Brusca, Frank. "The Dayton Cutoff." www.route40.net/page.asp?n=1073.

Buettner, Michael. "In Search of…the Dixie Highway in Ohio." February 2006. www.lincolnhighwayoh.com/v1/DixiePage2.html.

Gibson, Denny. "Dayton Cutoff Background." www.dennygibson.com/DayTrips/Trip15/background.htm.

———. *A Decade of Driving the Dixie Highway: Exploring the USA's First Highway System.* Cincinnati, OH: Trip Mouse Publishing, 2015.

———. "May 27, 2006: Dayton Cut Off." www.dennygibson.com/DayTrips/Trip15.

Harper, Glenn, and Doug Smith. *A Traveler's Guide to the Historic National Road in Ohio.* N.p., n.d. www.ohionationalroad.org/TravelersGuide/TravelersGuide.pdf.

Ohio History Connection. "Dayton and Covington Turnpike Company Account Book Page." ohiomemory.org/digital/collection/p267401coll32/id/13107.

Ronald, Bruce W., and Virginia Ronald. *Oakwood: The Far Hills.* Dayton, OH: Reflections Press, 1983.

Urban Ohio. "The Road to Sprawl: Interurban Suburbia…Carrmonte and Berkley Heights." June 17, 2006. forum.urbanohio.com/topic/2167-the-road-to-sprawl-i-interurban-suburbia-carrmonte-amp-berkley-heights.

Chapter 5

Gaffney, Timothy R. "Dayton, Ohio: Where All Nuclear Bomb Blasts Begin." *Dayton Daily News,* January 16, 2016. www.daytondailynews.com/news/opinion/dayton-ohio-where-all-nuclear-bomb-blasts-begin/oQEkVkZDB168m00rZIyc2O.

Gilbert, Keith V. "History of the Dayton Project." Monsanto Research Corporation. June 1969.

Medical News Today. "Polonium-210: Why Is Po-210 So Dangerous?" www.medicalnewstoday.com/articles/58088.php.

Thomas, Linda Carrick. *Polonium in the Playhouse: The Manhattan Project's Secret Work in Dayton, Ohio.* Columbus: Trillium, an Imprint of the Ohio State University Press, 2017.

U.S. Army Corps of Engineers. "Combined Preliminary Assessment/Site Inspection Report—Dayton Warehouse, City of Dayton, Montgomery County, Ohio, Revision 3." Prepared by URS Group, Inc., 2005.
———. "Site Inspection Report—Dayton Unit III, City of Dayton, Montgomery County, Ohio." Prepared by URS Group, Inc., 2004.

Chapter 6

Avdakiv, Steven, Deborah Griffin, Kathy Mast Kane and Nathalie Wright. "Ohio Modern: Preserving Our Recent Past, Dayton and Surrounding Area Survey Report." State of Ohio Historic Preservation Office, 2010.
Chanchani, Samiran. National Register of Historic Places Nomination for the Downtown Dayton Historic District. 2019.
City Plan Board, Dayton, Ohio. "Central Business District Study Outline." April 12, 1957.
The Danis Company. "Through the Years." danis100.com/Danis-Through-The-Years.
Flynn, Robert R., planning director. May 1, 1970. *Downtown Development Dayton*. City of Dayton, Dayton, OH.
Kappell, Jean. "A Little Bit of Heaven Right in Downtown Dayton." *Dayton Daily News*, July 8, 1976.
National Register of Historic Places Nomination for the Grant-Deneau Tower, 2016.
Peterson, D. *Graphic Presentations of Dayton's CBD with Emphasis on the Core, Historic and Proposed Block Designations.* July 1959. City of Dayton, Dayton, OH.
Urban Ohio. "'Center City West: Dayton Urban Renewal Continued." January 14, 2006. forum.urbanohio.com/topic/1171-quotcenter-city-westquotdayton-urban-renewal-continued.

Chapter 7

Allbaugh, Dave. "Work Set to Start at River's Edge Park." *Dayton Daily News*, February 25, 1979.
Babcock, Jim. "New to Depend on Old." *Dayton Journal Herald*, April 10, 1973.

———. "12M Rip Rap Road Project Scheduled to Begin in Mid-July." *Dayton Daily News*, June 29, 2000.

Batz, Bob. "Edge of Delight." *Dayton Daily News*, May 7, 1981.

Bechtel, James F. "Warehouse to Be Erected by Grain Dealers." *Dayton Daily News*, June 29, 1927.

Carlson, Bill. "Getting to Newfields Is Everyone's Problem." *Dayton Journal Herald*, April 10, 1973.

City of Dayton. *City of Dayton Public Arts Catalogue*. 2001.

Civil Defense Museum. "Standard Fallout Shelter Signs." www.civildefensemuseum.com/signs.

Cummings, James. "Newfields: The Plug Was Pulled on the Dream, but Residents Don't Seem to Mind." *Dayton Journal Herald*, July 17, 1979.

Dagley, Jen. "Newfields Streets Move from Blueprints to Mud." *Dayton Daily News*, October 31, 1973.

Dansker, Emil. "Connector Plan Dies in E. Dayton Meeting." *Dayton Daily News*, April 10, 1970.

Dayton Daily News. "Cheery Quarantine Hospital: Faces Cherry Hill, Burying Ground When Epidemics Killed Men 'Like Flies.'" January 31, 1932.

———. "City Thoroughfare Plan Would Cost $116 Million." February 6, 1968.

———. "Consequences Asked If Connector Unbuilt." April 15, 1970.

———. "Estimated 100,000 Birds Flocking in Small Area." February 28, 1949.

———. "Fire Hits Home, Kills Mrs. Shawen." August 17, 1956.

———. "First Tenants Chosen for Parkside Homes; Dedication Set Tuesday." July 20, 1941.

———. "Occupation of Parkside Homes Under Way after Ceremony." July 23, 1941.

———. "Old City Hospital Is Quarantine Center." June 21, 1943.

———. "One Hospital Here Not Overcrowded; In Fact, It Doesn't Have One Patient." January 8, 1950.

———. "Quarantine Hospital, Unused in Over Two Years, Ever Ready for Patients." December 15, 1935.

———. Special advertisement section. "Dayton Feed Plant in Full Production." May 27, 1945.

———. "To Assign Units to Tenants." July 3, 1941.

———. "To Slash Quarantine Hospital Costs." January 10, 1951.

———. "Use of Two City Institutions to Be Asked to Increase Obstetrical Facilities Here." August 23, 1942.

———. "We're Building a New Town." Advertisement. April 20, 1975.

Dayton Herald. "Care of Alcoholics for City Quarantine Hospital." March 22, 1952.

———. "City Makes Many Thousands on Real Estate Deal." October 7, 1915.

———. "New Venereal Hospital Open." June 22, 1943.

———. "Rapid Venereal Treatment Setup." May 9, 1944.

Dayton Journal. "Parkside Homes Low Rent Housing Project Opened." July 23, 1941.

Dayton Journal Herald. "C.E. Shawen, Home Donor, Doctor, Dies." August 28, 1951.

———. "Chicago Firm Buys Local Feed Company." April 1, 1945.

———. "Parkside Project to Open Tuesday; First Key Given." July 20, 1941.

Dillon, Pamela. "Spotlight: Public Art." March 24, 2002.

Dykes, David. "River Corridor Park Planners Want Amphitheater at Low Dam." *Dayton Daily News*, February 28, 1978.

Garloch, Karen. "HEW's Housing Concept Dies $21 Million Death." *Cincinnati Enquirer*, July 15, 1979.

Glover, Mark. "Newfields' New 'Pioneers' Optimistic about Future." *Dayton Daily News*, October 8, 1978.

Goldwyn, Ronald. "U.S. 35 Interchange Heading for Nowhere." *Dayton Journal Herald*, April 11, 1970.

Harty, Rosemary. "'It's Art!' 'That? It's Junk!' Either Way, It Cost $61,000." *Dayton Daily News*, June 6, 1989.

Hershey, William. "Board Seeks Help on 'Family' Matter." *Dayton Daily News*, March 13, 1974.

Historicbridges.org. "Rip Rap Road Bridge." historicbridges.org/bridges/browser/?bridgebrowser=ohio/oldriprap.

Huffman, Dale. "$7 Million Dead End Open in East Dayton." *Dayton Daily News*, October 20, 1971.

Kline, Benjamin. "Roads Ahead Look Smoother, Improved." *Dayton Daily News*, October 26, 2001.

Koehnen, Adele U. "Dayton-Area Family Recalls 'Pest House' on the Hill." *Dayton Daily News*, May 24, 1995.

Krebs, Betty Dietz. "Another Public Sculpture Challenges Old Definitions." *Dayton Daily News*, June 11, 1989.

Lamb, Kevin, and Lynn Hulsey. "The Park Nobody Wants to Use." *Dayton Daily News*, October 6, 1996.

Lippman, Andy. "Dream of City Dies as Roads Lead Nowhere." Associated Press. *Lancaster Eagle Gazette*, July 18, 1979.

McCall, Ken. "County Oks Bridge Project." *Dayton Daily News*, March 15, 2000.

McCaslin, Walt. "Newfields Plan Takes Shape." *Dayton Journal Herald*, November 29, 1974.

McKelvey, Vince. "Newfields Residents Won't Quit." *Dayton Journal Herald*, October 8, 1976.

Mendell, David. "Bridge Closed to Traffic." *Dayton Daily News*, May 3, 1997.

Montgomery-Greene County Civil Defense. "Community Shelter Plan for Montgomery-Greene Counties." Printed in the *Xenia Daily Gazette*, July 26, 1971.

Moore, Greg. "County to Spend $5 Million for 2,211 Newfields Acres." *Dayton Journal Herald*, September 13, 1978.

Nichols, Jim. "Newfields No Figment." *Dayton Daily News*, May 22, 1974.

Ownes, Bette. "Parts of Park at Newfields May Open in Year, State Says." *Dayton Daily News*, July 27, 1979.

Palfenier, Otto. "Samuel Puterbaugh." Geneology Page. gw.geneanet.org/ottopalfenier?lang=en&p=samuel&n=puterbaugh&oc=7.

Roth, Mark. "Newfields, HUD at Odds." *Dayton Journal Herald*, March 16, 1976.

Russ, Bonnie. "Social Problems to Be Anticipated." *Dayton Journal Herald*, April 10, 1973.

Schaaf, Liz. "Newfields Nightmare: An American Dream Is Near a Sour Ending." *Dayton Journal Herald*, January 29, 1979.

———. "Trotwood Looks at Merger Despite Pact with Dayton." *Dayton Journal Herald*, March 13, 1978.

Seiler, Michael. "Shelters…for Some." *Dayton Journal Herald*, February 25, 1971.

Sharkey, Mary Anne. "Newfields: Authority Is the Key to Making It More than Just a Development." *Dayton Journal Herald*, April 9, 1973.

Chapter 8

Babcock, Jim. "Network an Underground Operation." *Dayton Journal Herald*, March 23, 1981.

———. "Steam Heat." *Dayton Journal Herald*, March 23, 1981.

Carr, Ken. "Did You Know?" Dayton History Books Online. www.daytonhistorybooks.com/didyouknownov06.html.

Dayton Daily Herald. "Soldiers Home—The Great Underground Avenues." September 25, 1885.

Dayton Daily News. "Difficult Engineering Feat Accomplished in Construction of the Delco's New Tunnel." January 24, 1915.

————. "Greatest Improvement in the City's History." March 6, 1902.

Filby, Max. "Once Erased from the Map, Dayton VA Tunnel Could Be Reopened." *Dayton Daily News*, May 26, 2019. www.daytondailynews.com/news/local/once-erased-from-the-map-150-year-old-dayton-tunnel-could-reopened/TFHuOWpM5cE4mjGy26vF5M.

Gilette, Rich. "Dayton Building Has Rich History." *Dayton Daily News*, October 26, 2014.

Piqua Daily Call. "DP&L Steam Customers Escape Electric Rates, Gas Shortage." March 10, 1975.

Robinson, Amelia. "Where Is the Last Fragment of NCR's Famed Underground Dayton Tunnel System?" Dayton.com. March 15, 2019. www.dayton.com/news/special-reports/where-the-last-fragment-ncr-famed-underground-dayton-tunnel-system/Lziypn6qxHmJgpgtNBqgBJ/.

About the Author

Tony Kroeger is the planning division manager for the City of Dayton, where he has worked since 2006. He is a graduate of Miami University (bachelor's) and Clemson University (master's) in city and regional planning. He grew up in Cincinnati, Ohio, and came to Dayton from Greenville, South Carolina. He wishes to share his sense of wonder and excitement about cities with others, especially his children, Luke and Ben. He and his family live in the St. Anne's Hill historic district in Dayton. You can find him @tonykroeger on Twitter.

Visit us at
www.historypress.com
....